TO AFGHANISTAN AND BACK

ISBN 978-1-56163-359-3
© 2002 Ted Rall
Photos: © 2002 Judy Chang unless otherwise credited.

6th Printing

Library of Congress Cataloging-in-Publication Data
Rall, Ted.
   To Afghanistan and back / by Ted Rall.
      p. cm.
   ISBN 1-56163-325-9 (cloth)
      1. Afghanistan--Description and travel. 2. Afghanistan--History--2001-3. War on
Terrorism, 2001- I. Title.

DS352 .R25 2002
958.104'6--dc21

2002016537

TO AFGHANISTAN AND BACK

A Graphic Travelogue by

TED RALL

UPDATED EDITION

NANTIER · BEALL · MINOUSTCHINE
Publishing inc.
new york

Back Cover: The Kunduz front line near Khanabad. Photo: Judy Chang.

"Death and Boredom on the Front Line," "Taliban Family Values" and
"How We Lost the Afghan War" originally appeared in *The Village Voice*.

First, thanks are owed to David G. Hall at KFI Radio in Los Angeles and
Doug Simmons at *The Village Voice* for funding the trip chronicled in these pages.
Terry Nantier at NBM published this book; Martin Satryb art directed, and J.P. Trostle
did design and layout. David Stanford and Sue Roush at Universal Press Syndicate
edited the text. Sadoullo Khasanov of Mountain Travel Company Central in
Dushanbe got me into Afghanistan and, more importantly, got me out.

Contents

This is for
the people
who died.

Introduction

by Bill Maher

Shortly after the outbreak of hostilities in Afghanistan last October, award-winning cartoonist Ted Rall and his bride were deep in the heart of Pashtun country dodging 15,000-pound bunker-busters and haggling with locals over the price of drinking water so filthy a duck wouldn't shit in it. And you thought your second honeymoon was uninspired.

Taking pen in hand, Ted proceeded to skewer the insanity of the situation, not just with drawings but also with his prose, a series of dispatches as compelling and artfully rendered as anything I've read since...well, since *Dispatches*, Michael Herr's acclaimed book on his Vietnam War experiences. And while I don't always agree with Ted on the current conflict, the fact is he was there. Actually, Ted had traveled extensively throughout all the 'stan countries long before September 11th became a registered trademark. And since 9-11 he's seen, firsthand, what happens when a 5,000-pound precision-guided missile hits precisely the wrong target. Whereas the closest I've ever been to a genuine Afghan conflict was arguing prices with Akmed the rug salesman at this darling little boutique on Melrose.

Despite our occasional disagreements, Ted serves as a great guest on *Politically Incorrect*. Whatever our ideological differences, I know that when I pick up a book by Ted Rall my hackles will soon rise, my thoughts will be provoked, and my funny bone will be tickled. So good luck with the book, Ted, you revolting little America-hating pinko. And I mean that in the best possible way.

Bill Maher is host of the HBO show Real Time with Bill Maher.

Northern Alliance soldier, age 14.

Foreword

by Ted Rall

In 1933, the author Sherwood Anderson traveled throughout the United States. To get a sense of the national mood, he talked to everyone from factory owners to hobos about the Depression. He titled his resulting essay collection *Puzzled America*.

Though the circumstances are very different, America is puzzled again. Until now, terrorism has always been something that happened in other countries or that could be quickly forgotten. How could the richest, most powerful state ever created be caught so flat-footed? Why, after all the foreign aid we've sent to poorer nations, would anyone hate us so much? And who are 'they', anyway?

Visa issued by Northern Alliance.

Weeks after the 2001 suicide bombings of the World Trade Center and Pentagon, the people of the wealthiest nation on earth launched an intensive, high-technology bombing campaign against the poorest. U.S. policymakers were so unfamiliar with the region that the Central Intelligence Agency was forced to issue a public appeal for Americans fluent in Pashto and Tajik, yet these same people considered themselves qualified to radically restructure Afghanistan's fundamental culture and politics.

My agent Mary Anne Patey, my wife and I went to discover the results of our war upon ordinary Afghans. We never expected to find The Truth, because that's impossible. We did, however, attempt to separate propaganda from reality; in other words, to eliminate some of our puzzlement. This book is part of that effort.

Ted Rall, war correspondent. The Kunduz front is on the other side of the wall.

This book is told from my perspective (rather than jointly) for several reasons. First, Afghanistan's prevailing gender apartheid often caused me to have interactions that my female companions could not, and vice versa. Second, I was still so stunned by the intensity of my experience at the time of writing that I was lucky to be able to articulate my own thoughts, much less synthesize our communal experiences into a coherent group narrative format. Finally, as a reader I've always found single-person point-of-view easier to follow, particularly vis-à-vis the graphic-novel portion of this text.

All of us have friends and relatives who demanded to know why we risked traveling to a famously dangerous place, while carrying passports issued by a country then dropping bombs on the locals. My reply was always the same: "It's just a few weeks. Millions of people live there their entire lives."

Please think of them when you read this.

Ted Rall
New York City

1. Giving War
A Chance

So we're going to war against Afghanistan. Big deal. We've been at war with Afghanistan for years.

This New War is merely an escalation of genocide by trade sanction, this time with a few old-fashioned bombs and covert commando raids thrown in for popular effect. And while the explosions will look cool on cable TV news and the vague rumors of American death squads trekking through the mountains will sound dashing in a Rudyard Kipling-cum-Rambo kind of way, it will accomplish exactly nothing.

On the other hand, this brand of ham-fisted foreign policy ensures that America will never run out of enemies.

On September 24th, Secretary of State Colin Powell promised that the Bush Administration would finally cough up definitive proof of Saudi dissident Osama bin Laden's involvement in the suicide plane bombings of the Pentagon and World Trade Center: "I think in the near future, we will be able to put out a paper, a document, that will describe quite clearly the evidence that we have linking him to this attack."

For the sake of argument, let's assume that Powell is telling the truth: that bin Laden, and by extension his Taliban hosts in Afghanistan, financed, ordered or otherwise directly participated in the murder of 3,000 Americans.

Clearly, then, bin Laden ought to be hunted down and captured "dead or alive," in the John Wayne-informed lexicon of our appointed acting president. The Taliban should likewise suffer political capital punishment—being deposed by an overwhelming invasion force. Under military occupation, bin Laden's Al Qaeda network would be rounded up and shut down. Ditto for the training camps that educate terrorist wannabes for *jihad* against Western democracies. Within a year, cybercafes catering to backpacking college kids would spring up across Kabul.

Unfortunately, it won't make any difference. Most of the training camps for such radical guerrilla outfits as the Islamic Movement of Uzbekistan, which made a name for itself a few years back with its annual raids on southern Kyrgyzstan, are in Pakistan, Tajikistan and southern Kyrgyzstan. The Tajik and Kyrgyz governments are far too impoverished, politically weak and poorly armed to eject these insurgents, but both value their ten-year-old independence from the Soviet Union too much to allow foreign troops into their territory to do the job. *Madrassas* (religious schools) in the Baluchistan and Northwest Frontier Provinces of Pakistan continue to serve up Jihad 101, but the fragile military government of General Pervez Musharraf, ethnically aligned and beholden to the Taliban for battling the Indians in disputed Kashmir province, will never risk the wrath of Muslim extremists in their own country by shutting them down. Bottom line: bombing, destroying and militarily-occupying Afghanistan only shuts down a small fraction of the terrorist training facilities.

Now, let's escalate from the madness of an Afghan invasion (remember how well the same idea worked out for Britain and the USSR?) to full-fledged mayhem on a monumental scale. Assuming that we get the approval—and still better, military backing—of Russia's Vladimir Putin, U.S. troops could fan out across Central Asia. Tajikistan would come easy. Kyrgyzstan wouldn't require much effort. Pakistan is a nuclear state nowadays; perhaps we could pay them to close the *madrassas*.

It still wouldn't make much difference.

Tens of thousands of Arab fundamentalist militants have already graduated from those Taliban-affiliated training facilities. They're in Egypt, Saudi Arabia, Libya, the United Arab Emirates, Qatar, Syria...and Florida. They belong to dozens of distinct organizations, each enjoying individual sources of financing and adhering to separate

American F-16 preparing to bomb Bangi, Afghanistan.

goals and ideologies. Putting their alma maters out of business won't prevent them from carrying out future attacks on the U.S.

Nonetheless, it's always possible to carry a hypothetical war on terrorism to its logical extreme: somehow, perhaps using satellite surveillance and pixie dust, the U.S. and its allies successfully hunt down every single member of every militant Islamic organization in the world and either jail or kill them. Who knows how? Anyway—

It *still* wouldn't matter. Those dead and jailed militants have mothers, fathers, sisters and brothers. They have friends. And countless ordinary Muslim people would watch, driven to vengeance by the extraordinary ruthlessness of such a massive assault by America on individuals whose only proven sins are their beliefs. A new army of jihadists would rise from the ashes of Bush's 21st century crusade.

Nonetheless, America must have its vengeance. We're not the kind of people to sit around and mourn a few thousand dead office workers when there's some serious ass to kick. So we'll bomb or invade or something. It won't matter, but that doesn't matter. It's what we do.

Taliban POWs at the Taloqan town jail. The man at left claimed to be Uzbek—note the Uzbek hat—but guards said he was Pakistani. (Photo: Mary Anne Patey.)

2. The New Great Game

NEW YORK, October 9

Nursultan Nazarbayev has a terrible problem. He's the president and former Communist Party boss of Kazakhstan, the second-largest republic of the former Soviet Union. A few years ago, the giant country struck oil in the eastern portion of the Caspian Sea. Geologists estimate that sitting beneath the wind-blown steppes of Kazakhstan are 50 billion barrels of oil—by far the biggest untapped reserves in the world. (Saudi Arabia, currently the world's largest oil producer, is believed to have about 30 billion barrels remaining. Kazakhstan, meanwhile, may have unconfirmed reserves of up to 260 billion barrels.)

Kazakhstan's Soviet-subsidized economy collapsed immediately after independence in 1991. When I visited the then-capital of Almaty in 1997, I was struck by its utter absence of elderly people. One after another, Kazakhs confided that their parents had died of malnutrition during the brutal winters of 1993 and 1994. Middle-class residents of a superpower had been reduced to abject poverty virtually overnight; thirtysomething women who appeared sixtysomething hocked their wedding silver in underpasses next to reps for the Kazakh state art museum trying to move enough socialist realist paintings for a dollar each to keep the lights on. The average Kazakh earned $20 a month; those unwilling or unable to steal died of gangrene adjacent to long-winded tales of woe written on cardboard.

Autocrats tend to die badly during periods of downward mobility. Nazarbayev, therefore, has spent most of the last decade trying to get his land-locked oil out to sea. Once the oil starts flowing, it won't take long before Kazakhstan replaces Kuwait as the land of Benzes and ugly gold jewelry. But the longer the pipeline, the more expensive and vulnerable to sabotage it is. The shortest route runs through Iran but Kazakhstan is too closely aligned with the U.S. to offend it by cutting a deal with Teheran. Russia has helpfully offered to build a line connecting Kazakh oil rigs to the Black Sea, but neighboring Turkmenistan has experienced trouble with the Russians—they tend to divert the oil for their own uses without bothering to pay for it. There's even a plan to run crude out to the Pacific through China, but the proposed 5,300-mile line would be far too long to prove profitable.

The logical alternative, then, is Unocal's plan, which is to extend Turkmenistan's existing system west to the Kazakh field on the Caspian and southeast to the Pakistani port of Karachi on the Arabian Sea. That project runs through Afghanistan.

As Central Asian expert Ahmed Rashid describes in his 2000 book "Taliban: Militant Islam, Oil and Fundamentalism in Central Asia," the U.S. and Pakistan decided to install a stable regime into place in Afghanistan around 1994—a regime that would end the country's civil war and thus ensure the safety of the Unocal pipeline project. Impressed by the ruthlessness and willingness of the then-emerging Taliban to cut a pipeline deal, the U.S. State Department and Pakistan's Interservices Intelligence (I.S.I.) agency agreed to funnel arms and funding to the Taliban in their war against the ethnically Tajik Northern Alliance. As recently as 1999, U.S. taxpayers paid the entire annual salary of every single Taliban government official, all in the hopes of returning to the days of dollar-a-gallon gas. Pakistan, naturally, would pick up revenues from a Karachi oil port facility. Harkening to 19th century power politics between Russia and British India, Rashid dubbed the struggle for control of post-Soviet Central Asia "the new Great Game."

Predictably, the Taliban Frankenstein got out of control. The regime's unholy alliance with Osama bin Laden's terror network, their penchant for invading their neighbors and their production of 50 percent of the world's opium made them unlikely partners for the desired oil deal. Then-President Bill Clinton's 1998 cruise missile attack on Afghanistan briefly brought the Taliban back into line—they even eradicated opium poppy cultivation in less than a year—but they nonetheless continued supporting countless militant Islamic groups. When a group whose members had trained in Afghanistan hijacked four airplanes and used them to kill more than 3,000 Americans on September 11th, Washington's patience with its former client finally expired.

Finally, the Bushies had the perfect excuse to do what the U.S. had wanted all along—invade and/or install an old-school puppet regime in Kabul. Realpolitik no more cares about the 3,000 dead than it concerns itself with oppressed women in Afghanistan: this ersatz war by a phony president is solely about getting an oil pipeline deal done without interference from annoying local middlemen.

Central Asian politics, however, is a house of cards: every time you remove one element, the whole thing comes crashing down. Muslim extremists in both Pakistan and Afghanistan, for instance, will support additional terror attacks on the U.S. to avenge the elimination of the Taliban. A U.S.-installed Northern Alliance can't hold Kabul without an army of occupation because Afghan legitimacy hinges on capturing the capital on your own. And even if we do this the right way by funding and training the Northern Alliance so that they can seize power themselves, Pakistan's ethnic Pashtun government won't long stand the replacement of their Pashtun brothers in the Taliban by Northern Alliance Tajiks. Without Pakistani cooperation, there's no getting the oil out and there's no chance for long-term stability in Afghanistan.

As Bush would say, make no mistake: this is about oil. It's always about oil. And to twist a late '90s cliché, it's only boring because it's true.

3. Nineteen Guys Who Shook The World

"**P**ower is an illusion." columnist Jimmy Breslin wrote during Watergate. At no time in our lives has that truism been more evident.

NEW YORK, September 18

The demise of the Soviet Union, we know as surely as we can know anything nowadays, left us Americans in charge of the planet. What we never considered was how little it took to bring down our rival superpower: the C.I.A. dumping dollars on the floors of Moscow lavatories to destabilize the ruble. A nuclear meltdown at Chernobyl.

Afghanistan.

It happened to them. Now it's happening to us.

Integral to the shaking fists and flag-waving hysteria and the funerals—thousands and thousands and thousands more of those to come, by the way—is a rage born of impotence. Conservatives applaud and liberals deplore our expensive governmental monitoring systems—what would we have argued about had we known that neither the C.I.A. nor the N.S.A. knew what was going to go down September 11th? For what does it profit a country to starve its schools if its fattened Pentagon can't even protect *its own headquarters* from a terrorist attack?

The United States has finally been unmasked as the greatest Potemkin ever conceived—"great magnificent shapes, castles and kingdoms," in Breslin's words. Or to paraphrase Edward G. Robinson's classic dis of Fred MacMurray in "Double Indemnity": We thought we were smart, but we were wrong. We're just a little bigger.

Air-traffic controllers realized fairly quickly that those four jets had been hijacked. American Flight 11, out of Boston, took 46 minutes to hit Tower One of the World Trade Center. United Flight 175 struck Tower Two 65 minutes after leaving Boston. Most damning, American Flight 77 was aloft a total of 88 minutes—*nearly an hour and a half*—making it from Washington/Dulles to southern Ohio en route to Los Angeles before turning around. Math: the flight did a 180-degree turn at least 44 minutes away from the Pentagon. Why weren't our F-16s on top of that plane within 10 minutes? Why wasn't it shot down during the next 34 minutes after that? The answer, sheepishly admitted and buried deeply amid assorted tales of horror, was that there is no policy for forcing down a civilian airliner.

Unless, of course, there was. The Air Force denies shooting down United Flight 93, which crashed and burned in Shanksville, Pennsylvania, the government's silence certifying celled-in media stories of heroic passengers rebelling against their captors. Those accounts, however, are cast into doubt by the government's refusal to release the plane's voice cockpit recorder tapes to the public. It's a safe bet, after all, that a bold struggle for control would at least make it out in transcript form. So it's possible that Bush or other officials made a terrible, yet courageous, decision to act; if so, the need to keep it secret provides ample testimony to the aftermath of last year's election-that-never-was—if Bush is the perfect president for this time, he's the empty-headed embodiment of our national cluelessness.

America's embarrassment of embarrassments continues apace. C.I.A. superspooks admit that their posse of white Mormons from Utah never learned Pashto or Tajik, Afghanistan's two principal languages. The loss of four planes and a few days of airport closures decimates the biggest airline industry in the world, resonating through the economy in the form of the biggest stock-market crash ever. Half a dozen buildings accounting for less than one percent of New York City's office space vanish; the national economy plunges decidedly into recession and beyond.

What would we do if we really *were* at war? How can the richest superpower in the history of mankind have been brought so low by 19 guys?

The United States, it turns out, entered the 21st century atop a crumbling house of cards. When the Soviet Union went away, we lost the ideological and economic competition that had kept us sharp after World War II. We became complacent, smug and arrogant. History, Francis Fukuyama told us in 1993, had ended. Global free-market capitalism, epitomized and led by United States corporations, represented the pinnacle of achievement of historical evolution. A power vacuum opened in Central Asia. Afghanistan disintegrated into civil war, anarchy and religious madness. Surrounding republics—Uzbekistan, Kyrgyzstan, Tajikistan, Pakistan—were sucked into a vortex of instability and anti-Western sentiment fueled by clumsy U.S. attempts to suck all the oil out of the region without paying off any of the locals. This, and America's blank check to Israel, inspired tens of thousands of militant Muslims to their facile conclusion: Sometimes the bull in the china shop won't leave voluntarily. That's when you kill it.

Osama and his jihad boys sized us up fairly well. Behind the high-tech metal detectors in our airports were underpaid incompetents. Manning our tactical defenses were dimwitted dolts devoid of imagination. Bolstering our outsized economy was a mountain of debt and an easily-spooked securities market. And behind the boast that the World Trade Center could withstand a collision with a jet was the horrible, awful truth: no amount of bluster can annul the laws of physics. As the cliché goes, we believed our own hype and now we're paying the price.

Our close-to-the-bone brand of capitalism turned out to be our economic Achilles' heel. Corporations that fill metal tubes with highly-combustible fuel and upper-middle-

21

class citizens and propel them eight miles over the surface of the earth at high speeds ought to be prepared for an occasional mishap, but they're not—and neither are insurers who are, after all, in the business of risk appraisal. A week of reduced productivity has ruined crops (no crop dusters during the flight ban) and trashed the economies of states dependent on tourism. This, since George W. Bush and his tax-cutting maniacs have forgotten, is why governments and companies both need savings and surpluses. "It's my money," Republicans like to say, "and I can use it better than the government can." Worst of all, decades of increasing disparity of wealth has made it impossible for ordinary people to help out the only way they really could, by spending discretionary income. Now that we've let them steal all of our money, where are all the jobs rich people are supposed to create? This is the way empires end, with a bang and a whine.

4. Capitalism Comes to Central Asia

DUSHANBE, TAJIKISTAN, November 22

My fixer—no self-respecting Westerner does Central Asia without one, without a local to smooth his way—tried to take me to the Hotel Dushanbe. But I'm no sucker. I didn't let the big rooms or working boilers seduce me.

"Take me to the Hotel Tajikistan!" I insisted to Sadoullo. An anguished look crossed Sadoullo's face: "But it's...cheaper."

In Tajikistan, as back home in Manhattan, cheap means bad. But here in the waning days of the Afghan war rush, the Hotel Tajikistan is *the* place to be. Dushanbe, the worn-out capital of the most-failed of former Soviet Republics, sight of a not-unlike-Afghanistan civil war during the '90s, is the jumping-off point for anyone who wants to get into Afghanistan, a country with no international airport. And the Hotel Tajikistan has become a Scene: There are more "journos" in the lobby than in the entire *New York Times* building.

When you catch Christiane Amanpour and the rest of the talking heads broadcasting from the roof of the Islamabad Marriott in Pakistan, know this: People who don't know jack about this part of the world go to Pakistan to get into Afghanistan. You would, too, if you looked at a map: the Khyber Pass offers the best geographical connector between Afghanistan and the outside world. But the Pakistani-Afghan border has been closed since U.S. bombs started falling; the closest thing to actual action is interviews with Afghan refugees at camps in Peshawar and Quetta.

Tajikistan has received remarkably little coverage in America's New War, as cable TV news calls it. When the Taliban still ruled, the Tajik-dominated Northern Alliance used the country as a supply

Tajik press card, required to enter the restricted zone near Afghanistan.

23

line—opium paste and emeralds out, guns in. Even when the Islamic State of Afghanistan controlled just five percent of the country, the Alliance ran a regular helicopter shuttle between Dushanbe and Faizabad, Afghanistan. Now, that chopper and government-sponsored journalist convoys have become the only reliable routes in and out of the land of the mujaheddin.

"Are you with a relief agency?" a thinned-lipped 50ish lady from Seattle asks me in the elevator, obviously sizing up my suitability for a middle-of-nowhere one-nighter.

"Journalism," I reply, "talk radio and *The Village Voice.*"

"Ohhhh," she says.

We both know what that "oh" means.

The aid agency workers, mainly Christians and retro-granola types, consider the journalists vultures of the lowest order, gleefully snapping pictures of gore and cruel acts. The laptop and video-feed set look at the aid workers with a mix of pity and contempt, for they believe their efforts are both pointless (feeding a few thousand while millions starve) and self-interested (converting Muslims to Christianity).

Both are right. The real winners here are the Afghans and Tajiks sufficiently educated in English and the ways of the marketplace to exploit the army of expense-account-funded scribblers and proselytizers in their midst.

Refugee passing a bombed-out Afghan village, Kunduz Province. (Photo: Mary Anne Patey.)

The Northern Alliance charges $550 for a one-way helicopter ride that takes 20 minutes; to increase revenue they sell twice as many tickets as there are seats and let Darwinistic fisticuffs work out the difference. The same experience, minus the double booking, cost just $130 a year ago. English/Dari/Pashto translators go for more than $100 a day in a nation with an average monthly income of $1.40. Even a 20-mile taxi ride, at most a buck a year ago, will set back the accounting department at CNN $40 or more.

According to the Afghan embassy, a few hundred journalists are running around inflating the Afghan economy; every week, roughly 40 to 80 more enter the country. The war hasn't been completely gentrified, however: the car convoy, which travels some of the worst mountain roads anywhere on the planet "for eight or nine hours, or maybe three days," according to my fixer, costs a mere $400 per car. Before the war you could've done the same thing for $80.

"I just hope the Taliban hold out at Kunduz." I overheard a guy from German Channel 4 say in the elevator here at the hotel. Many residents of Dushanbe feel the same way.

Taking a break at the front.

5. Death and Boredom on the Front Line

TALOQAN, AFGHANISTAN, November 25

Afghans are different from you and me. We live in a world in which more people are alive than have ever lived and died. Theirs is the diametric opposite. Afghanistan is defined by things that used to be: people, ideas, Buddha statues, cities. Journalistic hyperbole has no place here: even the most abused adjectives fall short in a country where Soviet tank treads serve as speed bumps. The poor are poorer than words can describe, the anarchy of armed-to-the-teeth 11-year-old soldiers more prevalent than anyone would care to admit, the destruction so complete that, as upon viewing the Grand Canyon for the first time, the brain can't process the quantity or perfect genius of the horror.

Like "Three Kings" come to life, this third Afghan war is characterized by surreal boredom, for locals and foreigners alike, with a dash of genuine death tossed in just to keep things interesting.

Nowhere is this truer than in the provincial capital of Taloqan. Dozens of Western journalists, a few from the country that started this whole thing, scurry about this town, captured by the Northern Alliance just days ago, wallowing in inanity as they place bets on their own chances of coming home alive.

"So," my new neighbor, who rode a Northern Alliance tank into Taloqan for *The Washington Post*, asks me seconds after my arrival, "What are you doing for power?"

Laptops and satellite phones and short-wave radios have us paying taxi drivers $20 a shot to drain their car batteries, running foul-smelling generators over the four-day road trip over the Tajik border, and endlessly clicking the annual rechargers from REI. Lost in the lust for direct current is the oft-told yet incomprehensible statistic of the average salary—$1.40 per month—and even paying the $20 to recharge the phone isn't pushing that buck-forty very far.

"Who's your translator?" is the second question any Euro will ask you, because a bad translator can cost you both your story and your life. A good one, on the other hand, doesn't have to speak English. He fixes things with the Foreign Ministry so that you can go to the front, scores you a cheap rental car—ideally with a cigarette lighter so you can recharge your sat phone—and finds you food during the diurnal Ramadan witching hours.

At night, the bombs come.

The siege of Kunduz, which is important because the place sits at the intersection of two of the five paved highways in the country, rages 20 miles to the west. Mostly the bombs, big 5,000-pounders according to Saloqhan, a jovial Northern Alliance commander who briefs me each morning, fall on the Taliban sector of Kunduz. One night a bridge vanishes; the next a residential neighborhood goes up with nary a mention on American television.

"We don't care if we get killed," an Uzbek fighter named Khalev reassures me as he poses with his shiny AK. "What is important is to bomb the foreigner Taliban so they will come out and we can kill them." And the collateral damage? "It should not be mentioned as it would cause Americans to doubt themselves."

Ever since the Taliban defenders of Kunduz reneged on their surrender offer with a ferociously lethal ambush of their would-be conquerors, the Alliance has adopted a nationalist stance: Afghan Taliban will be welcomed into the warm bosom of indefinite imprisonment, while Pakistanis, Chechens, and other foreign volunteers will be executed *en masse*.

Donald Rumsfeld's obscene statement that the U.S. is happy to take no prisoners in Afghanistan is taken seriously by Afghans of all political persuasions. "As long as we are alive," I hear a Taliban commander inside Kunduz tell his Alliance counterpart over a military radio, "we will fight."

"You should surrender to prevent more killing," his Alliance counterpart reasons.

"Your killing or my killing?" the Taliban officer closes.

Sometimes the bombs hit the residential neighborhoods of this Northern Alliance-held city. It's intellectual calculus of the lowest sort. The per capita odds of you yourself getting hit by a bomb are tiny, akin to winning the lottery or getting that big promotion. And yet every night the bombs come again.

The important thing is to leave your windows open. It gets very cold at night, around 20 or 30 degrees, but there isn't any heat anyway. At first the ground shakes; then a rush of air punches the windows. A Swiss radio journalist is at the Red Crescent Hospital next door having shards of glass extracted from his body. "That's what happens when you don't leave the window open," his convoy mate, a writer for the British newspaper *The Guardian*, smirks. Twenty-four hours later the Brit is in the same hospital, unlikely to survive an encounter with Taliban P.O.W.s he was interviewing.

The journalists have reasons to be fatalistic: we're dropping like flies. Three killed, then four carjacked and killed by the Taliban near Jalalabad a week ago, then three more. None were killed in battle, Ernie Pyle-style. All were carjacked or mugged. The Alliance helps by turning us into targets: they force us into caravans of rented vehicles containing hundreds of thousands of dollars in cash, traveling across remote dustscapes, with no more control on human behavior than the estimated five million mines planted among the spindly trees alongside the road.

When the sun comes up nine and a half hours ahead of and a thousand years behind Ground Zero, the war commute begins. Tanks and trucks and Japanese rental cars with Dubai plates zoom west across the desert, dodging donkeys, potholes, piles of wheat drying on the asphalt—and every now and then, a group of refugees from Kunduz. The drama is purely theoretical: in practice the sight of teenage girls in brightly colored dresses, toting ridiculously tiny bags containing everything they own, becomes instantaneously mundane. Likewise the front itself, which has become such a local institution that it now has its own parking attendants for visiting journos.

Self-proclaimed experts on the differences between the various kinds of mines speculate on the F-16 circling the hamlet of Bangi, just outside Kunduz. "He's not going to drop," bets Lance from the BBC. "Once they drop they establish a straight line and get the hell out of there." If you squint, you can make out a Taliban bunker a half mile down the valley on a perfectly sunny day. "They've been trying to hit us all day," Lance notes. "They know we're here."

Lance is right. After a few hours photographing and sketching Alliance troops, the heat gets to me, and I hop into my car for the drive back to Taloqan. On the way home, I call my mom to wish her a happy Thanksgiving.

A few minutes after leaving Bangi, the Taliban score a coup: they take out the journalists' parking lot. Some guy from Finnish radio comes back in a pickup truck, bleeding from pebbles and rocks lodged somewhere inside him. And after that, all hell breaks loose when a Taliban commander drives down the road to surrender himself, a pile of guns, and a Ford Expedition.

There's a scramble for the keys to the SUV booty: 25 Northern Alliance soldiers are wounded and one is killed in the ensuing fracas. But the visceral thrill that normally pairs up with such brushes with death is oddly absent. In just 24 hours, the place where I was standing a few minutes earlier is pulverized by mortar shells, and the town I'm living in is

Journalist convoy becomes bogged down, rural Takhar Province. (Photo: Mary Anne Patey.)

randomly bombed by Air Force dipshits. Mostly, though, it's a mind-numbingly dull existence. For one thing, I engaged in mere tourism where the locals are born pro. For another, the advantages of life over death aren't quite as apparent here as they are back home.

In the evening they send us back to T-town. "You should go home," Alliance commander General Mohammad Daoud informs the assembly of dehydrated writers and cameramen after another day when the main camera-ready action on the front has been an exchange of bodies.

"What are these guys dying of, old age?" someone asks. We want blood, Robert Capa, soldiers falling back dramatically, arms splayed. The closest we get is puffs of smoke in the distance where people and buildings used to be and a camel blown to smithereens by a mine. "We want to stay for the bombing," I tell Daoud. "We've been waiting for hours."

"If you stay after dark," he warns, "some of my troops will rob you. And maybe worse." There's something tantalizing about this possibility. For one thing, I'd have something to write about. For another, it might jump-start emotions and bowels locked solid by days of fending off stooped old ladies in burqas pulling at my clothes in Central Asia's ultimate form of aggressive panhandling. Maybe the sight of all of those guns— every other male carries at least one, too many of them pointed at me—might spark my sympathy for the millions who lie under graves of stones and green flags hanging limply from mangy sticks. More likely, some dumb fuck would shoot me just for the hell of it. I don't care to be Number 11, not tonight.

So I go home to a dinner of butter biscuits from Qatar with a side of Ashi-Mashi orange cola, and wait for the bombs to come.

6. All Things Fall Apart

TALOQAN, AFGHANISTAN, November 29

One week after the Taliban fled this dusty provincial capital to join their comrades defending nearby Kunduz, freedom was in the air. Eleven-year-old boys toting rocket launchers bigger than themselves milled about the central square, playing soccer, flying kites and shooting their AKs into the air. Women briefly lifted their burqas to take a clear look at the workman painting over the Taliban logo on the local school.

I wandered the streets feeling more like Mick Jagger than a citizen of the nation dropping bombs on the locals; a throng of men and boys followed me as I made my way to the market to buy Nescafé and flea powder. Due to Ramadan, the bazaar is quiet during the day, but the Shah Massoud restaurant springs to life at night. The local specialty is Afghan steak kebabs mixed with eggs (like the country itself, they're interesting but dangerous).

In a scene straight out of the Wild West, scowling gunmen sprawl over the tables, their weaponry laying about as they sing along to Indian movie music blasting from a loudspeaker and occasionally engage one another in fisticuffs. It's hard to believe that just a week ago most of these men were Talibs.

"Of course we will throw away our burqas," a young woman told me at the bazaar, "but we are afraid the Taliban will come back. If they do, they will punish anyone who removes their *burqas*."

There is understandable uncertainty in the air about whether "the current government," as locals call it, will stay in power. But it's more than that. Women as well as men dread a return to the "Mad Max"-like state of anarchy that characterized the early '90s, when the Northern Alliance last ruled this country.

From the April 1992 deposal of President Mohammad Najibullah until 1996, when the Taliban dragged him out of a U.N. compound and castrated, shot and hanged him, the Northern Alliance's Islamic State of Afghanistan was less a government than a state of institutionalized chaos. The highways were trolled by rapists and warlords, and the cities became so unsafe that few Afghans dared venture out after dark.

During this period, Afghanistan secured its role as the world's leading supplier of heroin. The Taliban put an end to all that, but at a terrible price—the rule of law found its pinnacle at 3 o'clock Friday afternoons when criminals were taken to the soccer stadium east of Kabul and subjected to amputation, stoning and execution.

The bad old days, it seems, may be coming back. At this point, the sole expression of government authority here is a lone traffic policeman standing at the Pakistani-style rotary in the middle of the main intersection. By yesterday, even he had repaired to a disused ammunition dump nearby where he could be found fast asleep, a lit cigarette dangling from his lips. Half of the male population—the heavily armed half—is cruising the streets looking for people to rob. And the drug trade has made a remarkable overnight comeback; pure opium paste is selling briskly a few blocks off the main drag.

The American bombing campaign, which continues to take a toll on Kunduz and much of Takhar Province, has heightened the sense that there are no longer any rules.

I confronted one of the customers at the opium joint: "Isn't that illegal in Afghanistan?"

"Nothing is illegal in Afghanistan," he replied. "You can do whatever you want and no one cares."

"That's not always true," I suggested, recalling week-old history.

"The Taliban would have cared," he responded, grinding the paste into fine dust and sprinkling it into a cigarette. "But you Americans have gotten rid of them, and now we are free."

32

Northern Alliance soldiers take a break from the Battle of Kunduz. (Photo: Maryanne Patey.)

Certainly the Taliban's purist vision of Islam has taken a beating. Though people are faithfully fasting during Ramadan, nary a head turns in response to the mullahs' call to prayer. Alcoholic beverages have become the hottest consumer item in town.

"What? You didn't bring wine?" my guide and "fixer" asked me last night, as he geared up for a night of opium-induced haze.

"All the western journalists bring wine from Tajikistan," he scolded. Along with the collapse of legality and religiosity has come a wholesale plunge into the kind of societal cynicism that could mean real trouble if and when the new (and old) Northern Alliance gets its act together.

"In this country it's hard to tell the difference between life and death," the wine aficionado told me between bites of laghman noodles. "So we might as well live a little between all the dying."

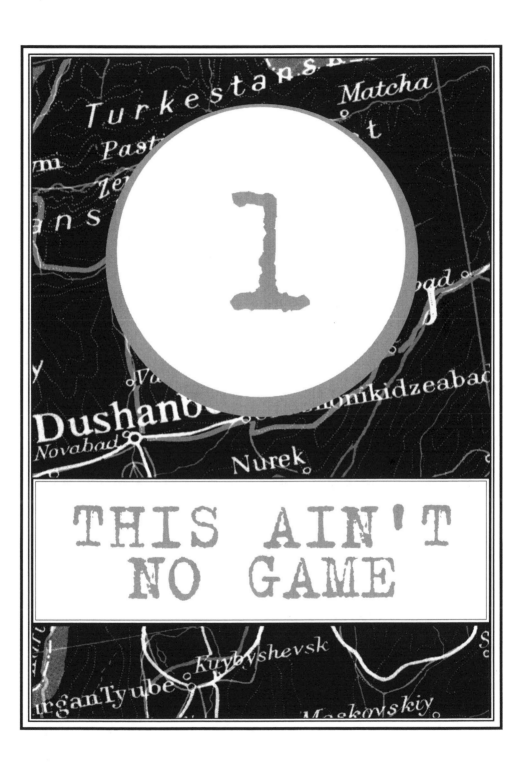

1

THIS AIN'T
NO GAME

THE GUY JUST WOULDN'T SHUT UP.

I NEVER GO ANYWHERE WITHOUT A BULLETPROOF VEST... GOT ONE?

NAH. THEY DON'T COVER MY FAVORITE PARTS.

MY JOURNALIST CONVOY LEFT FOR THE AFGHAN BORDER AN HOUR LATER.

THE HOTEL TAJIKISTAN WASN'T MUCH, BUT I KNEW I'D MISS THE OVERFRIED EGGS. DUSHANBE HAD NEVER SEEMED SO CIVILIZED.

GET ONE! THE $400 MODELS WILL BARELY STOP A 9-mm; THEY WON'T DO SHIT AGAINST AN AK. YOU GOTTA SPEND AT LEAST 3 GRAND!

EVERY ADVENTURE STARTS LIKE THIS. THEY TOLD ODYSSEUS TO STAY HOME, TOO.

JUST DON'T GO. THE MOUNTAIN PASSES ARE ALL SNOWED SHUT UNTIL MAY. MY GUY NEARLY GOT SNOWED IN FOR THE WINTER!

CBS' NEWS DIRECTOR HAD BEEN A PERFECT EXAMPLE. HIS AFGHAN CORRESPONDENT HAD OBVIOUSLY SOLD HIM A LOAD OF CRAP TO JUSTIFY THE MONEY HE WAS GETTING. KNOWING BETTER MADE ME FEEL BETTER ABOUT HEADING TO AFGHANISTAN AS AN AMERICAN CITIZEN.

MOST OF THE PASSES ARE OPEN ALL YEAR... IDIOT!

AS I'D FLOWN FROM TURKEY TO TAJIKISTAN, SOME TALIBAN HAD MURDERED AND GANG-RAPED A FRENCH REPORTER.

OCTOBER WAS WEIRD. BUSH'S DAD HAD COZIED UP TO OSAMA BIN LADEN, BUT NOW THE SON WAS BLAMING HIM FOR THE SUICIDE ATTACKS. RATHER THAN NEGOTIATE FOR EXTRADITION, THE U.S. OPTED TO BOMB THE TALIBAN OUT OF POWER.

THE **EVIL ONE** LIVES IN A **CAVE**. **THAT'S** HOW EVIL THE EVIL DOERS ARE!

FLAGS COVERED CARS, BUSES, WINDOWS, PEOPLE. BUSH'S 90% POPULARITY RATING WASN'T GOOD ENOUGH FOR A NATION MOURNING ITS LOST SENSE OF INVULNERABILITY.

EITHER YOU'RE WITH OUR COMMANDER-IN-CHIEF, OR YOU'RE A TRAITOR!

AS IT HAD DURING THE '80s, THE CULTURAL AND IDEOLOGICAL CLOCK TURNED BACK TO THE '50s. McCARTHYISM—EVEN OVERT RACISM—WAS BACK.

IF SOMEONE EVEN **LOOKS** ARAB, THEY SHOULDN'T FLY.

NOW I UNDERSTAND WHY THEY STUCK JAPS IN CAMPS.

THE PRESIDENT PROMISED TO LIE TO US, AND THE MEDIA PLEDGED TO GO ALONG.

WE WON'T DO ANYTHING TO JEOPARDIZE THE SUCCESS OF MILITARY OPERATIONS.

AMER NEW WAR

WHEN THE DEMOCRATS LET REPUBLICANS DELIVER "THE DEMOCRATIC RESPONSE" TO BUSH'S SPEECH, IT SENT A CLEAR MESSAGE:

THERE *IS* NO OPPOSITION.

WORLD WAR II-STYLE PROPAGANDA POSTERS APPEARED.

★ UNITED ★ WE STAND

WANTED

GONE BUT NOT FORGOTTE

I HADN'T CHANGED. I DID THE SAME SNARKY CARTOONS AND COLUMNS AS BEFORE, BUT BEING MYSELF WAS GETTING DANGEROUS.

I DON'T RECOGNIZE THE ADDRESS... THINK IT'S 'THRAX?

41

I COULDN'T STAND WATCHING THIS ON TV... I KNOW THEY'RE LYING TO US.

DEFINITELY... BUT HOW AND HOW MUCH?

HOTEL TAJIKISTAN, DUSHANBE

PAKISTAN HAD CLOSED ITS BORDER WITH AFGHANISTAN TO EVERYONE BUT SMUGGLERS, CRIMINALS AND FLEEING TALIBS. THIS MADE TAJIKISTAN THE ONLY WAY IN.

CHINA

KASHMIR

IRAN

AFGHANISTAN

PAKISTAN

45 JOURNALISTS, MOST OF THEM EUROS, LEFT FOR THE BORDER ON A BLUSTERY NOVEMBER MORNING. THE MEDIA PECKING ORDER WAS ESTABLISHED RIGHT AWAY. THE TV GUYS LUGGED MOUNTAINS OF METAL BOXES IN BIG NEW SUVs. RADIO AND PRINT TRAVELED LIGHT, IN SOVIET-MADE LADAS. THE BBC BROUGHT ITS OWN WHITE ARMORED JEEP. I SCORED A VOLGA SEDAN WITH WINDOWS THAT WOULDN'T OPEN; I DID SLIGHTLY BETTER THAN AVERAGE.

I WANTED TO COVER THE HUMAN ANGLE: HOW PEOPLE LIVED, THE EFFECT OF THE WAR ON ORDINARY LIVES. MY COLLEAGUES, ON THE OTHER HAND, WERE CHASING SCOOPS.

I WANT TO BE THE FIRST TO LIBERATE KUNDUZ!

FUCK THAT! SKY TELEVISION HAS DIBS ON KUNDUZ!

STILL, WE WERE ALL WAR TOURISTS, OSTENSIBLY THERE TO TELL THE TRUTH TO THE WORLD. IN REALITY, WE WANTED THE TRUTH FOR OURSELVES.

THINK THEY'LL BOMB OUR CONVOY?

NO WAY—THE AMERICANS ARE VERY PRECISE.

NONE OF MY FELLOW JOURNOS HAD BEEN TO AFGHANISTAN BEFORE.

HOW COULD THE BORDER BE *CLOSED*? IT CLOSES AT 6, BUT IT'S ONLY 4!

THEY WANT US TO CROSS AT NIGHT SO THEY CAN SHAKE US DOWN. IT'S STANDARD.

NIGHT FELL INSTANTLY, AT 5. A TOLERABLE DAYTIME 40° PLUNGED INTO SINGLE DIGITS. TRAPPED BY THE RUSSIAN BORDER PATROL IN THE TAJIK-AFGHAN NEUTRAL ZONE, WE WARMED OURSELVES OVER AN IMPROMPTU BONFIRE AND MARVELED AT THE STARS.

THE MILKY WAY! IT'S A BAR OF LIGHT... NOT JUST A VAGUE FUZZ LIKE IN AMERICA...

A FULL MOON REFLECTED OFF THE PYANJ RIVER. ON THE OTHER SIDE, THE LIGHTS OF AFGHAN VEHICLES MOVED SLOWLY. I SENSED A PLACE THAT LOOKED INTERESTING DURING THE DAY, BUT THERE WAS NO WAY TO KNOW FOR SURE.

THEY LET US ONTO THE BARGE AT MIDNIGHT. A MODIFIED TRACTOR BOLTED TO THE DECK PULLED A CABLE THAT SPANNED THE PYANJ. ACCORDING TO THE RUSSIANS, THE WATER WAS OFTEN TOO CHOPPY TO ALLOW THE BORDER TO REMAIN OPEN.

ABC NEWS

44

AN HOUR LATER, I WAS THE LAST KID PICKED FOR KICKBALL. EVERYONE WAS GONE EXCEPT FOR ME AND THE DRIVER OF AN '80s-ERA RUSSIAN PICK-UP.

OK—I TAKE $40, BUT IT SHOULD BE $1,400.

IT SHOULD BE $1 AND YOU KNOW IT.

I SOON ARRIVED AT A HALF-FINISHED GUEST HOUSE OWNED BY A LOCAL COMMANDER. I WAS FIRST; ALL THE OTHER DRIVERS HAD DRIVEN THEIR FARES IN CIRCLES TO JUSTIFY THEIR $800 FEES.

MY ROOM DEFINED SPARTAN: IT CONTAINED DUST ON A CEMENT FLOOR. NO CARPET, NO FURNITURE, NO LIGHT, NO HEAT.

MY FIRST AFGHAN VILLAGE LIT UP IN MY HEADLIGHTS. A TALIBAN JET HAD LEVELED IT TO EARTHEN MOUNDS JUST A FEW DAYS EARLIER. A TRASHED SOVIET TANK SERVED AS A SIGNPOST; ITS TREADS WERE NOW A SPEEDBUMP. THE ROAD WAS MORE HOLE THAN NOT.

I FELT MY BODY TEMPERA-TURE DROPPING AS THE NIGHT CRAWLED BY. I TURNED FROM MY BACK TO MY SIDE TO MINIMIZE THE SURFACE AREA AGAINST THE COLD FLOOR, BUT IT DIDN'T DO MUCH TO HELP.

I CAN'T TAKE ANOTHER 3 WEEKS OF THIS SHIT... I'LL DIE OF PNEUMONIA.

THE ROAD STRETCHED ACROSS AN ENDLESS EXPANSE OF DESERT, OCCASIONALLY INTERRUPTED BY SLOW CLIMBS THROUGH STEEP PASSES. HUNDREDS OF FEET UP WERE BUSH'S FAMOUS CAVES, BUT THERE WAS NO WAY TO KNOW WHETHER ANY OF HIS "EVIL ONES" WERE LURKING, WAITING TO SEND US OFF TO MEET ALLAH.

IF ANYONE'S WAITING FOR US, THEY'LL SEE US COMING FOR MILES.

YOU JUST COULDN'T OUTRUN A BULLET, ESPECIALLY NOT ON ROADS LIKE THIS. IF SOME BANDIT WANTED TO ROB YOU, THEY'D HAVE ALL THE TIME IN THE WORLD. YOU'D BE LUCKY IF THEY DECIDED TO LET YOU LIVE.

JOVID WOULDN'T LEAVE ME ALONE ABOUT TRANSLATING.

I AM $120 PER DAY. THE CURRENT GOVERNMENT SETS THE PRICE. OK THEN?

I DIDN'T BELIEVE HIM. HOW COULD THE NORTHERN ALLIANCE SET SUCH A PRICE IN A NATION WITH A $1.40/MONTH AVERAGE INCOME?

I IGNORED JOVID, FIGURING THAT I'D GET A SMARTER, CHEAPER TRANSLATOR IN THE METROPOLIS OF TALOQAN. MEANWHILE, I CHATTED UP THE BRIT.

YOU'RE NOT LIKE OTHER AMERICANS I KNOW.

IS THAT AN INSULT?

2

COMMUTER WAR

THE BRIT WAS RIGHT. THE WOMEN OF TALOQAN WERE STILL WEARING BURQAS.

IS IT LIKE THIS EVEN IN KABUL?

EVERYWHERE. A FEW TOOK 'EM OFF FOR THE CAMERAS, FOR A MINUTE, FOR A DOLLAR.

TALOQAN, A MID-SIZED PROVINCIAL CITY THAT WAS HOME TO PERHAPS 50,000 SOULS, HAD BEEN SURROUNDED BY NORTHERN ALLIANCE SOLDIERS A WEEK EARLIER. THE AMERICANS DROPPED BOMBS UNTIL THE TALIBAN COMMANDERS LED THEIR TROOPS OUT TO SURRENDER.

SALAAM.

SALAAM. I AM *SO* SORRY.

THE PRISONERS IMMEDIATELY BECAME DEFECTORS. THE ERSTWHILE TALIBS RUSHED TO THE KHANABAD BAZAAR ACROSS THE STREET FROM A PARK WHERE THEY'D PREVIOUSLY GATHERED TO WATCH THIEVES BEING AMPUTATED AND CHEATING WIVES AND HUSBANDS STONED TO DEATH. THEY PAID 20,000 AFGHANIS (40¢) TO GET THEIR BEARDS SHAVEN; $1 BOUGHT A *PAKUL*, THE NURISTANI BERET MADE FAMOUS BY ASSASSINATED NORTHERN ALLIANCE GENERAL SHAH MASSOUD. LESS THAN 24 HOURS LATER, THE CLEAN-SHAVEN EX-TALIBS WERE FIGHTING ALONGSIDE OTHER NORTHERN ALLIANCE TROOPS WHO THEMSELVES HAD DEFECTED EXACTLY THE SAME WAY EARLIER.

ON THE ONE HAND, THE AFGHANS CHANGED SIDES SO OFTEN THAT IT WAS IMPOSSIBLE TO KNOW THEIR TRUE OPINIONS.

ON THE OTHER, IT WAS QUITE POSSIBLE THAT THEIR ONLY TRUE LOYALTIES WERE TO THEMSELVES AND THE MOMENT.

POK POK POK POK

YESTERDAY WAS YESTERDAY. TODAY IS TODAY.

POPULAR AFGHAN PROVERB

EVEN JOURNALISTS WITH NO INTEREST IN THE SIEGE OF KUNDUZ WERE STUCK IN TALOQAN. THE PROBLEM WAS CARTOGRAPHIC: TALOQAN SITS AT THE EASTERN TERMINUS OF ONE OF AFGHANISTAN'S 5 PAVED ROADS, THE EAST-WEST HIGHWAY THAT ULTIMATELY GOES ON TO HERAT ON THE IRANIAN BORDER, AFTER PASSING THROUGH KUNDUZ AND MAZAR-E-SHARIF. THE NORTH-SOUTH ROAD TO KABUL CROSSES THE EAST-WEST ARTERY AT KUNDUZ.

KUNDUZ

To Taloqan

HERAT

HINDU

SALONG TUNNEL

KUSH

☒ TALIBAN AREA
▬ PAVED HWY.
▭ UNPAVED RD.

KABUL

UNTIL THE KUNDUZ BOTTLENECK OPENED UP, THE MEDIA WOULD BE WAITING IN TALOQAN.

To Kandahar

YOU COULD GO AROUND KUNDUZ, BUT THE ROADS ARE SO BAD AND SO LONG THAT YOU'D HAVE TO SPEND 2 OR 3 NIGHTS IN YOUR VEHICLE — BECAUSE THE VILLAGERS WON'T ALLOW STRANGERS TO STAY WITH THEM. SLEEPING OUTDOORS MEANS CERTAIN RAPE AND DEATH AT THE HANDS OF SOLDIER-BANDITS.

AT THE NORTHERN ALLIANCE'S FOREIGN MINISTRY, A HARRIED MUJAHEDEEN OFFICIAL USING FURNITURE BLENDING AFGHAN MINIMALISM AND BAROQUE BLAXPLOITATION FILM AESTHETICS TOLD JOVID TO TAKE ME TO A GUEST HOUSE ACROSS THE STREET FROM A RED CRESCENT HOSPITAL.

THANKS FOR TRANSLATING, BUT I CAN'T AFFORD $120 A DAY.

THE PRICE IS SET. YOU MUST PAY.

AFGHAN HOMES ARE PERFECTLY ADAPTED TO A CULTURE WHERE HEAVILY-ARMED THUGS ROAM THE STREETS. A HIGH WALL, TIPPED WITH BROKEN GLASS OR BARBED WIRE, LINES THE STREET. A STURDY DOOR, USUALLY REINFORCED WITH SEVERAL LAYERS OF THICK METAL TO BLOCK BULLETS AND SUPPORTED BY A MEDIEVAL-STYLE DOOR JAM, OPENS TO A COURTYARD.

THERE ARE TYPICALLY TWO SMALL HOUSES INSIDE, ONE FACING NORTH FOR SUMMER LIVING AND ANOTHER FACING SOUTH OR WEST FOR WINTER. CONSTRUCTION IS USUALLY MUD-ADOBE, COVERED BY A THINLY-THATCHED ROOF SUPPORTED BY BEAMS MADE FROM THIN ASH TREES. SMALL VEGETABLE GARDENS AND A POSSE OF CHICKENS AND ROOSTERS ARE STANDARD.

TO STREET
OUTHOUSE
GARDEN
WINTER HOUSE
SUMMER HOUSE
N

MY ROOM WAS 7'×10'. THE WINDOW WAS BROKEN. THE PROPRIETORS HAD PATCHED THE HOLES IN THE WALL WITH POSTERS OF DUBAI OFFICE BUILDINGS. DUBAI DIDN'T LOOK LIKE MUCH FUN.

THE CARPET ON THE FLOOR WOULD HAVE SOLD FOR $2,000 IN NEW YORK IF NOT FOR ITS RESINOUS GRIME, HOLES AND AN INFESTATION OF VORACIOUS FLEAS. I DISCOVERED THE SCORPIONS LATER.

MR. T EXPERIENCE AND THE WOMEN

SURROUNDING THE CARPET WERE A FEW FUTON-LIKE PADS FOR SLEEPING. LIKE THE COUNTRY'S SOUL, THE PADDING HAD BEEN RUTHLESSLY CRUSHED.

TWO REPORTERS FROM *THE WASHINGTON POST* LIVED ACROSS THE HALL. ONE OF THEM HAD FAMOUSLY BECOME THE FIRST REPORTER INTO TALOQAN, HAVING RIDDEN IN ON A TANK.

THE FRONT WAS ROUGH TODAY— HEY! WHAT ARE YOU DOING FOR POWER?

THE QUEST FOR ELECTRICITY WAS ENDLESS. SATELLITE PHONES, LAPTOPS, DIGITAL CAMERAS, ALL THE TOOLS NEEDED TO SEND COPY TO EDITORS AND PRODUCERS, RUN ON RECHARGEABLE BATTERIES.

NO, I *CANNOT* REPEAT THAT. REPEATING THINGS COSTS ME A BUCK A WORD!!

FORTUNATELY, 3 PORTUGESE TV REPORTERS NEXT DOOR HAD A GENERATOR. UNFORTUNATELY, LOW-GRADE AFGHAN PETROL KILLED THE GENERATOR.

A JANITOR AT THE RED CRESCENT HOSPITAL RAN A RECHARGING BUSINESS, BUT YOU RARELY GOT A FULL CHARGE FOR YOUR MONEY. AND THE HOSPITAL COULD BE A DANGEROUS PLACE.

$10. COME BACK IN 2 HOURS.

ON THE WAY BACK FROM THE HOSPITAL ONE MORNING, AN AMBULANCE BEARING A WOUNDED TALIB PULLED UP.

PITAL

A FEW MINUTES LATER:

BOOM

BLOOD, GRISTLE AND BROKEN GLASS LITTERED THE STREET AROUND THE BACK OF THE AMBULANCE. THE P.O.W. HAD LET OUT AN "ALLAH AKBAR" BEFORE DETONATING A COUPLE OF GRENADES. HE ALSO KILLED THE DRIVER.

WHEN I GOT MY PHONE BACK, IT WAS ONLY A QUARTER CHARGED. NONETHELESS, THE JANITOR DEMANDED THE WHOLE TEN BUCKS.

MY GUEST HOUSE HAD NO WATER, LIGHTS, OR HEAT. IF YOU WANTED WATER, YOU HAD TO PAY FOR IT. HOT WATER WAS MORE. NO MATTER HOW MUCH YOU PAID, THOUGH, YOU WERE COLD AND MISERABLE AND DIRTY MOST OF THE TIME.

THAT'D BE GREAT. THANKS!

I WILL BOIL WATER FOR YOUR *HAMAM*.

PLEASE PAY ME $5 NOW.

MY HOT BATHS, EVEN IF THEY INVOLVED DOUSING MYSELF WITH A RUSTY OIL CAN IN A DARK SHED FULL OF MUNITIONS, OFFERED A RARE MOMENT OF SERENITY AS CHOPPERS FLEW A FEW HUNDRED FEET OVERHEAD. BUT I STILL NEEDED THE STANDARD CHINESE-MADE COLEMAN-STYLE HURRICANE LAMP USED BY AFGHANS TO LIGHT AND WARM THEIR HOMES.

I HEADED TO THE BAZAAR.

THE LAMP PRESENTED A NIGHTLY DILEMMA. WHICH IS WORSE: POISONING BY BENZENE FUMES OR FREEZING TO DEATH?

MY EYES ARE BURNING.

DON'T COMPLAIN— LOOK AT THE CIRCLES AROUND MY FLEA BITES. I BET I'VE GOT LYME'S.

JOVID SHOWED UP WITH A DRIVER IN THE MORNING FOR MY DAILY WAR COMMUTE.

ANY INFORMATION ABOUT KUNDUZ?

THEY SAID THAT YESTERDAY.

THE FOREIGN MINISTRY SAYS IT WILL FALL TODAY.

YES, BUT NOW THEY'RE CERTAIN.

AL-AMHED ROCERIES S

IF KUNDUZ FALLS, WHERE DO YOU WANT TO GO?

MAZAR-E-SHARIF, THEN HERAT, THEN KABUL. WANNA COME?

JOVID WAS A DORK, BUT HE WAS ONE OF THE FEW HONEST AFGHANS I'D MET. AND HIS DRIVERS COST ONLY $50 A DAY.

AFTER THE MORNING BRIEFING AT GENERAL DAOUD'S COMPOUND, WE'D DRIVE TO THE FRONT.

THERE ARE MORE REFUGEES THAN USUAL TODAY.

THERE WAS A LOT OF AMERICAN BOMBING LAST NIGHT.

I KNOW.

TANKS AND ARMORED PERSONNEL CARRIERS EN ROUTE TO THE FRONT CRUSHED WHEAT DRYING ON THE ROAD, PASSING TRUCKS FULL OF TIRED TROOPS RETURNING TO TALOQAN. F-16s CIRCLED; SOMETIMES THEY BOMBED CARS JUST FOR THE HELL OF IT.

WHO CARED ABOUT ANOTHER BODY EXCHANGE? AS I HEADED FOR MY CAR, A COMMOTION STIRRED AMONG THE SOLDIERS. A TALIBAN COMMANDER HAD DECIDED TO DEFECT.

SALAAM.

SALAAM. DO YOU HAVE A GIFT FOR ME?

THE SOLDIERS COULDN'T CONTAIN THEMSELVES. THEY RAN TO THE TALIB'S SUV.

OH, SHIT— THE DUMBASS LEFT HIS KEYS IN THE IGNITION!

AT LEAST 100 TROOPS CLIMBED OVER EACH OTHER TRYING TO GET IN. A FEW TALIB POWs THREW THEIR AKs INTO THE CROWD TO SATE THEM, BUT IT WAS POINTLESS.

PAK PAK PAK PAK

ULTIMATELY, A GRENADE PROVED THE DECISIVE FACTOR.

CLICK

WHEN THE SMOKE CLEARED FROM THE BATTLE OF THE FORD EXPEDITION, 25 NORTHERN ALLIANCE TROOPS HAD BEEN SHOT. ONE, A 16-YEAR-OLD KID, WAS MORTALLY WOUNDED.

BOOM

THEY *COULD* WAIT FOR HIM TO DIE BEFORE STEALING HIS CLOTHES.

THE TALIBAN WERE DESCRIBED AS A RAG-TAG MILITIA, BUT THE NORTHERN ALLIANCE WASN'T ANY BETTER. THEY WERE KIDS WITH NOTHING TO DO, TRAINED FOR BANDITRY BY THEIR DADS IN A NATION WITH 90% UNEMPLOYMENT.

I CAN'T AFFORD A UNIFORM. BUT IF I HAD THE MONEY FOR A UNIFORM I'D SPEND IT ON NEW BOOTS.

EVEN MILITARY HEIRARCHY WAS IMPOTENT. GENERAL DAOUD ADDRESSED US FRONT-LINE REPORTERS.

LEAVE BEFORE DARK OR MY TROOPS WILL ROB YOU.

THEY SEEMED NICE ENOUGH FOR NOW, BUT I DIDN'T DOUBT THAT THAT WOULD CHANGE AFTER DARK.

LIFE IN A WAR ZONE IS LIKE WORKING AS A SECURITY GUARD OR FIREFIGHTER. MOST OF THE TIME, NOTHING HAPPENS. BUT WHEN IT DOES, ALL HELL BREAKS LOOSE.

THE TALIBAN HAD BEEN SIMPLE-MINDED, CRUEL HICKS. BUT THEY'D BROUGHT LAW AND ORDER. NOW THAT THE NORTHERN ALLIANCE HAD RESTORED ANARCHY, ONE COULDN'T HELP BEING DISGUSTED AT THE AFGHANS FOR TOLERATING THESE THUGS.

AFGHANISTAN WAS LIKE THAT. WITHIN A FEW DAYS YOU GOT USED TO THE FACT THAT PEOPLE WERE SHOOTING PROJECTILES ALL AROUND YOU.

PAK PAK PAK

AURAL PSYCHOLOGY IS A STRANGE THING. GUNFIRE KILLED THOUSANDS, BUT THE SOUND WAS SO SMALL—LIKE FIRECRACKERS—THAT THE HUMAN BRAIN COULDN'T PROCESS THE DANGER THAT IT REPRESENTED.

SHE DIDN'T FAINT. SHE CAUGHT A STRAY.

BOMBS EVAPORATED DOZENS OF PEOPLE EACH, YET THEY WEREN'T SCARY. AGAIN, IT WAS A SOUND THING: UNLESS YOU WERE DIRECTLY UNDER ONE, IT SOUNDED LIKE SOMEONE PUNCHING A PILLOW.

PLOOF PLOOF PLOOF

THAT'S ACROSS THE SQUARE.

ONE NIGHT AROUND 8, I THOUGHT THAT BUSH HAD LOST WHAT LITTLE MIND HE HAD TO BEGIN WITH. THE EARTH SHIFTED BACK AND FORTH TWICE. A BLAST OF AIR PUNCHED THE WINDOW.

ONE OF THE POLES NEXT DOOR GOT A WINDOW BLOWN INTO HIS CHEST.

CONTRARY TO THE PROPAGANDA BACK HOME, THE U.S.A.F. BOMBED ANYTHING AND EVERYTHING. YOU'D THINK THAT PREDICTABILITY WOULD MAKE BEING BOMBED WORSE, BUT IT DIDN'T. MOST RAIDS RAN FROM 6 TO 9:30 PM.

IT'S ODDLY PRETTY.

THE NEXT MORNING:

LAST NIGHT, THAT WAS A SPECIAL 15,000-POUND BOMB. IT DESTROYED A BRIDGE IN KUNDUZ.

IT FELT LIKE A NUKE!

KUNDUZ WAS 22 MILES AWAY.

I'D ALWAYS WONDERED HOW PEOPLE SURVIVED MASS BOMBINGS, LIKE DURING THE BLITZ, WITHOUT LOSING THEIR MINDS. NOW, I THINK I KNOW.

IT'S LIKE A NATURE SPECIAL I SAW. THOUSANDS OF WILDEBEEST MIGRATE ACROSS THE AFRICAN PLAINS. THEIR ROUTE TAKES THEM ACROSS A RIVER INFESTED WITH HUGE CROCODILES. I DON'T KNOW WHY THEY DON'T SIMPLY GO AROUND THE RIVER. MAYBE THEY CAN'T; MAYBE THEY DON'T THINK ABOUT IT.

ANYWAY, IF YOU BELIEVE THE NARRATOR, THE WILDEBEEST ENGAGE IN A COLD CALCULUS. SOME OF THEM WILL GET EATEN, BUT THE VAST MAJORITY WON'T. IT'LL SUCK FOR THE VICTIMS, BUT THE ODDS OF YOU YOURSELF AS AN INDIVIDUAL WILDEBEEST MAKING IT ARE EXCELLENT. SO YOU ALL HOP IN, IGNORING THE CHURNING BLOODY WATER AROUND YOU... UNLESS, OF COURSE, YOU YOURSELF ARE THE SOURCE OF THAT BLOOD.

BOMBING IS LIKE THAT. EVEN WHEN THEY'RE COMING EVERY 30 SECONDS, CHANCES ARE THAT YOU'LL LIVE TO SEE MORNING. THERE ARE SO MANY PEOPLE TO BOMB AND RELATIVELY SO FEW BOMBS TO HIT THEM WITH. WHY BOTHER TO LEAVE?

BOMBING LOTTO: IT'S A COPING MECHANISM FOR INSANITY.

LIFE AT MY GUEST HOUSE WAS FILLED WITH A MILLION MUNDANE DILEMMAS. WOULD MY HOSTS THINK I WAS RUDE FOR SPRINKLING WHITE FLEA POWDER ON THEIR RED CARPET? WOULD IT WORK?

DON'T DO THAT! IT'S IMPOLITE.

UM..OK.

CRISIS ARRIVED IN THE FORM OF A REP FROM THE FOREIGN MINISTRY.

WE HEARD THAT YOU ARE UNHAPPY HERE.

THAT WAS TRUE, BUT I HADN'T SAID ANYTHING TO ANYONE. ANYWAY, I WOULD'VE TAKEN AN ARMED GUARD OVER A NEW ADDRESS.

WHY?

WE'RE MOVING YOU. YOUR NEW HOUSE IS FAR SUPERIOR. IT EVEN HAS ELECTRICITY!

IT WAS A DIFFICULT CHOICE. THE NEW PLACE WAS 3 TIMES BIGGER, BUT BECAUSE IT WAS A NORTH-FACING SUMMER HOUSE IT WAS $20°$ TO $30°$ INSIDE.

IS THERE ANY WAY TO MAKE IT WARMER?

WE'LL ADD ANOTHER CARPET.

ELECTRICITY, THOUGH IT ONLY WORKED 3 HOURS A DAY, WAS A MAJOR INCENTIVE SINCE I'D BEEN PAYING $20 TWICE A DAY TO CHARGE MY SAT PHONE FROM PEOPLE'S CAR BATTERIES. ON THE OTHER HAND, THERE'D BE NO MORE FELLOW JOURNOS IN THE SAME COMPOUND.

IT'S VERY NICE. I'LL LET YOU KNOW.

IT WAS A BIG ISSUE: 3 MORE JOURNALISTS HAD BEEN MURDERED, AGAIN ON THE KABUL-JALALABAD HIGHWAY.

8? WHY ARE THEY STILL ONLY REPORTING 8 DEAD?

KLIK

KLIK

SOLITUDE COULD BE DEADLY.

IT WASN'T THAT WE WEREN'T ALL MORE WILLING TO DIE THAN OTHER PEOPLE. WAR CORRESPONDENTS MAY OR MAY NOT *WANT* TO DIE, BUT THEY ALL NEED TO STAY ALIVE TO DO THEIR JOBS. THE TRUTH IS: THEY WORK HARD TO STAY ALIVE WHILE THROWING THEMSELVES INTO SITUATIONS SANER PEOPLE AVOID.

I NEED YOU IN SRI LANKA FOR 4, MAYBE 5, WEEKS.

OK.

A FRENCH TV CHICK HAD SUMMED IT UP NICELY BACK IN TAJIKISTAN.

I DON'T MIND GETTING KILLED IN BATTLE, WHILE GETTING A STORY. GETTING OFFED FOR MY MONEY, THOUGH—WHERE'S THE GLORY IN THAT?

EACH REPORTER USED A DIFFERENT APPROACH TO SURVIVING THE AFGHAN HUNTING PARTIES. SOME HIRED COMMANDERS AS THEIR PERSONAL BODYGUARDS, THOUGH GUNMEN OFTEN ROBBED THEIR EMPLOYERS. OTHERS NEVER WENT ANYWHERE WITHOUT A CONVOY.

I ALWAYS FAVORED GOING IT ALONE. YOU ATTRACT LESS ATTENTION THAT WAY. BUT LONE WOLVES GOT NOTICED IN AFGHANISTAN TOO. WHO WOULD WATCH MY BACK IF I MOVED?

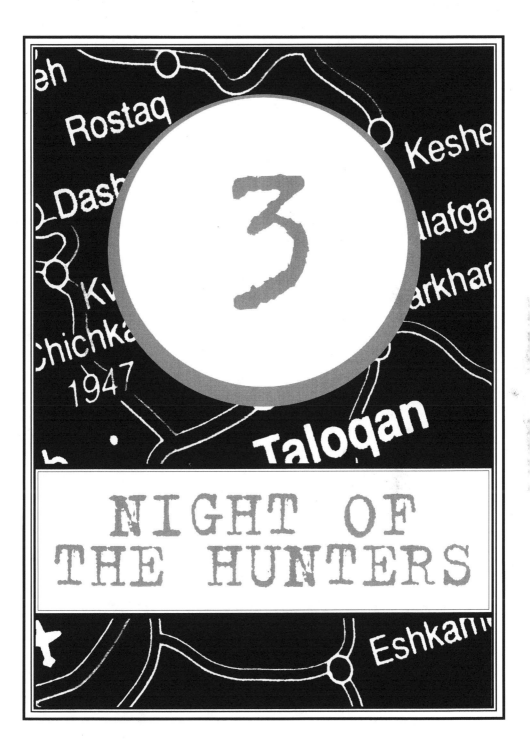

3

NIGHT OF THE HUNTERS

IN THE END, MY HOUSE'S OVERPAID GOFER JAMSHID MADE MY DECISION FOR ME. WHEN I GOT UP THE NEXT MORNING THE PORTUGESE WERE UP IN ARMS.
DO YOU KNOW WHERE HE GETS THE WATER FOR OUR *HAMAMS*?
YEAH. THE WELL.
NO! HE'S BEEN DRAWING OUR BATH WATER FROM THE **CHANNEL!**
THE "CHANNEL" WAS THE GUTTER ON THE SIDE OF THE ROAD. LOCALS WASHED IN IT. THEY ALSO SHAT IN IT. IT WAS CHALKY AND VILE AND FULL OF LITTER AND DONKEY TURDS.
NOW THAT YOU MENTION IT, THERE WERE LEAVES IN THE WATER YESTERDAY.
DO YOU HAVE A RASH TOO?
EVERYONE HAD GRAYISH RED WELTS AROUND THEIR WAISTS.
I THINK THESE ARE FROM FLEAS.
I TRIED NEGOTIATING WITH JAMSHID.
SHE'S GOING TO KILL YOU UNLESS YOU PROMISE TO USE WELL WATER FOR OUR *HAMAM*. OK?
YES. SURE.
DON'T "YES, SURE" ME. ARE YOU 100% SURE YOU'LL NEVER USE CHANNEL WATER AGAIN?
NO.

THE OUTCOME OF THE WAR HAD SEEMED INEVITABLE UNTIL 500 TALIBAN ESCAPED FROM PRISON AND BROKE INTO AN ARMS CACHE IN MAZAR-E-SHARIF. A CIA AGENT NAMED JOHNNY SPANN, WHO'D BEEN INTERROGATING THE POWs, HELD THEM OFF FOR HOURS BEFORE RUNNING OUT OF AMMO. 2,000 U.S. MARINES CROSSED THE UZBEK BORDER FROM TERMIZ TO CRUSH THE REBELLION. AND AS USUAL: BOMBS. LOTS AND LOTS OF BOMBS.

THE NEWS RIPPLED EAST. TALIBAN "CELLS"—IN REALITY, NORTHERN ALLIANCE SOLDIERS WHOSE ALLEGIANCES HAD SWITCHED BACK AS EASILY AS THEY'D DEFECTED—SPRUNG UP IN BANGI AND DASHT-E QA'LEH. IN TALOQAN, OUR 45 – WELL, 43 – JOURNALISTS BLITHELY CONTINUED THEIR WAR COMMUTE TO THE KUNDUZ FRONT. WOMEN VANISHED FROM THE STREETS. A WORK-MAN STOPPED PAINTING OVER THE TALIBAN LOGO ON THE TOWN SCHOOL. THE NORTH WAS IN PLAY.

I'D BEEN TREATING MYSELF TO POST-RAMAZAN DINNERS AT THE SHAH MASSOUD RESTAURANT (PREVIOUSLY THE MULLAH OMAR). EVERYONE WAS ARMED AND FRESH FROM THE FRONT, SO YOU GOT RESPECT MERELY FOR SITTING DOWN. IT WAS THE ONLY PLACE WHERE I ENJOYED LOCAL PRICING: 30¢ FOR ALL THE BREAD, KEBABS AND CHAI YOU COULD STAND.

CHAI?

NE.

I STOPPED GOING TO THE SHAH MASSOUD AFTER MAZAR. FACES SCOWLED; OTHERS LEERED. ANYONE COULD KILL YOU WITHOUT BEING PUNISHED; I DIDN'T WANT TO PUSH IT.

76

NOTHING WAS WHAT I'D EXPECTED. THIS WAS, NATURALLY, WHY I'D COME IN THE FIRST PLACE: TO SEPARATE REALITY FROM WAR-FEVER PROPAGANDA. STILL, THAT DIFFERENCE WAS DISCONCERTING: IN A 99% MUSLIM NATION THAT USED THE KORAN IN PLACE OF A LEGAL CODE, HARDLY ANYONE PRAYED. OPIUM WAS SOLD—AND CONSUMED—OPENLY. AND THE BAZAARS SOLD VIDEO CD PORN TO THRONGS OF SELF-DESCRIBED MUSLIM FUNDAMENTALISTS.

"THOUNDERS BOOBS"* IS EXCELLENT!

MY WIFE AND I FOUND THE PLOT TURGID AND UNFULFILLING.

* YES, THEY REALLY SPELLED IT THAT WAY.

ONE EVENING MY LANDLORD SCORED ME A COPY OF "TERMINATOR 2". UNFORTUNATELY, THE ELECTRIC CURRENT WAS SO WEAK, THE IMAGE REPEATEDLY PIXELATED AND LOOPED BACK TO THE BEGINNING OF EACH SCENE. NONETHELESS, IT WAS GREAT TO LOSE MYSELF IF ONLY FOR A LITTLE OVER AN HOUR.

DIDN'T WE ALREADY SEE THIS SCENE?

TWICE.

FOR THE FIRST TIME SINCE I'D ARRIVED IN AFGHANISTAN, I DIDN'T DREAM.

BAM
BAM
BAM

WHAT IF ONE OF THE PORTUGESE NEEDED SOMETHING? MY NEW LANDLORD RAN A PHARMACY; COULD SOMEONE FROM THE HOSPITAL NEED SOME DRUGS?

I CHECKED MY WATCH. WHO THE HELL WOULD KNOCK ON MY DOOR AT 3 IN THE MORNING?

IT SOUNDED LIKE 3 OR 4 MEN. THEY WERE INSISTENT; THEY POUNDED LOUDER AND LOUDER. THE LONGER THEY POUNDED, THE MORE I WAS TEMPTED TO OPEN THE DOOR. BUT IT WASN'T MY PLACE TO JEOPARDIZE AN ENTIRE FAMILY—AND IT WASN'T MY HOUSE.

FINALLY, THEY WENT AWAY.

ASSHOLES! NOW THEY'VE GOT THE ROOSTERS GOING.

ARR
ARR
PACKA
LOO!

I WAS ROLLING UP MY BAG WHEN PEDRO RAN IN, WEARING A STONE-COLD SERIOUS EXPRESSION.

LAST NIGHT SOME SOLDIERS KILLED ONE OF THE SWEDISH TV GUYS. EVERYONE'S LEAVING.

THE SWEDES LIVED 3 DOORS DOWN, NEXT DOOR TO THE POLES AND RUSSIANS. I'D SEEN THEM AT DAOUD'S PRESS CONFERENCES AND AT THE FRONT.

HOW'D IT HAPPEN?

3 OR 4 GUYS KNOCKED ON HIS DOOR. WHEN HE OPENED IT THEY SHOT HIM. THEY'D HAVE KILLED HIS 5 ROOMIES BUT THEIR TRANSLATOR BEGGED FOR THEIR LIVES.

THE NORTHERN ALLIANCE AND THEIR U.S. PUPPETMASTERS HAD A FIRMLY MONSTROUS POLICY: NO ASSISTANCE TO JOURNALISTS, INCLUDING MEDEVACS. THEY SENT EMPTY CHOPPERS BACK TO TAJIKISTAN ALL THE TIME; STILL, THEY REFUSED TO SPARE ANY OF THAT EXTRA SPACE FOR THE SWEDE'S COFFIN. THUS THEY CONDEMNED HIS BODY TO THE DESECRATION OF 10 HOURS ON PITTED AFGHAN ROADS.

AT LEAST THEY BACKED DOWN ON THE $2,000.

IT ONLY TOOK AN HOUR TO DISSOLVE MY LITTLE COMMUNITY. I FIRED MY DRIVER, MY TRANSLATOR AND THE BOY WHO FETCHED MY CHAI. I NOTIFIED MY LANDLORD AND ENGAGED IN THE USUAL LEASE-BREAKING ARGUMENTS.

HE SAYS YOU SHOULD PAY $15 EXTRA FOR THE HAMAM.

THAT WAS INCLUDED IN THE $15 I ALREADY PAID!

I TIPPED MY TRANSLATOR $200, MY BENZENE LAMP AND A HOT-WATER THERMOS. THEN I ASSIGNED HIM TO FIND ME A TRUCK FOR THE EVACUATION.

WE SHOULD LEAVE NOW, BEFORE THE OTHER JOURNALISTS. IF SOMEONE IS WAITING TO AMBUSH US, THEY'LL EXPECT A WHOLE CONVOY.

TRUE. AND GET US A CRAPPY SOVIET TRUCK. WE WANT TO LOOK LOCAL.

I HAVE THE PERFECT DRIVER. HE USED TO WORK FOR THE TALIBAN; HE WON'T STOP FOR ANYONE.

GREAT. START WITH $200 AND PAY HIM $300 IF YOU HAVE TO.

IT WAS JUST A SIMPLE BOX, ITS TOP COVERED WITH A GREEN TARP, AND IT DIDN'T SEEM TO AFFECT MY FELLOW TRAVELLERS. PEOPLE TALKED. OTHERS LAUGHED AT A JOKE I DIDN'T HEAR. THE BBC WERE THEIR USUAL SELVES.

ROIGHT— WE HAVE TO GET OUR JEEP ABOARD THIS BARGE. SOMEONE NEEDS TO SCOOT OVER THIS COFFIN, ROIGHT?

45 PEOPLE HAD ENTERED AFGHANISTAN. ONLY 42 LEFT. THE OTHERS WOULD NEVER AGAIN EAT A MEAL, REPORT A STORY, MAKE LOVE, OR WONDER WHAT THE PYANJ LOOKED LIKE UNDER A BRIGHT YELLOW SUN.

THE CHEESEBALL AT THE HOTEL TAJIKISTAN HAD BEEN RIGHT AFTER ALL. ULF STROMBERG *HAD* COME HOME IN A BOX, BUT IT COULD JUST AS EASILY HAVE BEEN ANY— OR ALL— OF US.

YOU COULD BE GOING HOME **IN A BOX**!

I KNEW THAT I'D NEVER AGAIN FEEL INVULNERABLE. THE TEENAGER INSIDE ME WAS DEAD. BUT THE GUY HAD BEEN WRONG ABOUT SOMETHING ELSE.

U.S. NATIONAL

◄ BAGGAGE CLAIM
◄ PASSPORT CONTROL
◄ CUSTOMS

7. Taliban Family Values

For several weeks the little boy soldiers and journalist war tourists lurked at a curve in the highway a few kilometers east of Kunduz, waiting for things to open up. American bombs had driven the Taliban and their law-and-order-at-any-price mores to their southern redoubt in Kandahar. All that stood in the way of the Northern Alliance becoming the government of North Afghanistan was an estimated 30,000 diehard Talibs holed up in the otherwise uninteresting provincial capital down the dusty road.

KHANABAD, AFGHANISTAN, December 5

Modern warfare, even in preindustrial Afghanistan, requires asphalt. The road that goes west from the Northern Alliance stronghold of Taloqan to Kunduz continues on to Mazar-e-Sharif, the largest city north of the Hindu Kush. The Alliance needs Mazar in order to get U.S. weapons and troops across the Uzbek border at Termiz, and to run supplies down to Kabul and west to Herat on the Iranian border along the nation's main highway, the A76—one of the five paved roads in the whole joint. You need Kunduz to keep Mazar to keep Kabul to keep from becoming the main event at someone else's mass-execution fiesta.

Traditional Afghan treachery kept the siege entertaining. One Taliban surrender offer after another was followed by torrents of gunfire aimed at their would-be conquerors. "This unacceptable behavior is the influence of the Pakistanis, Chechens, and other foreign elements among the Taliban," Alliance general Daoud announced sternly. "These Arabs will be sent before a judge and executed."

This being Afghanistan, where the only truth is that everything is a lie, nothing of the sort occurred. The Pakistanis flew back home, possibly to rejoin Osama bin Laden's beleaguered but well-funded posse (most Afghans believe that he fled to Kashmir months ago, more likely than not with the help of the C.I.A.), causing many Western media types to wonder aloud whether the Alliance was maturing into the kind of realistic entity that could govern and unify this quintessentially unruly place. Afghans, on the other hand, recognized their new government slipping back into its old ways. Once again, lawlessness, even murder, was going utterly unpunished.

Before George W. Bush decided to avenge September 11th by reordering the Afghan

85

Women in Burqas, Khanabad. Despite Western news reports, Afghan women continued to wear their veils under Northern Alliance rule.

political landscape with daisy-cutter bombs, the Northern Alliance was an internation-ally recognized government with hardly any territory to its name. President Burhanuddin Rabbani's Islamic State of Afghanistan had presided in Kabul from 1992 until the 1996 rise of the Taliban, but constant civil war between Rabbani and two war-lords, Abdul Rashid Dostum and Gulbuddin Hekmatyar, caused even more devastation than the Soviet war and plunged the country into anarchy.

Though at the price of personal freedom, most famously for the women who were transformed into null social factors, the Taliban's fierce brand of discipline was wel-comed by most Afghans when they pushed Rabbani's gang into internal exile in Badakhshan province in the mountainous northeast near the Chinese border. Most peo-ple expected the Taliban to finish off the Alliance and its five percent share of real estate by 2002 at the latest. World Trade, saturation bombing, and the traditional preternatu-ral ability of Afghans to react to changing times with instantaneous personal reinvention turned that 95 to 5 equation upside-down in just a month. The Northern Alliance did-n't so much conquer Afghanistan as buy it with your tax dollars.

Despite the usual human rights concerns, a few hundred P.O.W.s executed here and there, Alliance troops mainly behaved themselves fairly decently by the admittedly lenient national standards. Even the renewal of factional infighting between Rabbani and Dostum over which army would rule Kunduz after the Taliban departed involved more words over tea than impressive explosions. The question was: Would that decorum devolve into the "Mad Max"-esque mayhem of the early '90s? And given how the Alliance came to capture so much of the country by simply having Talibs hit their local barber shops and trade in their turbans for Ahmad Shah Massoud trademark Nuristani hats, would the Alliance become Talibanized or vice versa, and what would any of it mean?

Even as shells were still flitting about Kunduz's main drag and dawdling Talibs were holding out at the airport three miles away, the answer became clear: In the New Afghanistan, anything goes. Kunduz's newly liberated bazaar, always a festival of free-wheeling capitalism in Central Asia, instantaneously assumed an even more manic tone. Until November 26, the notoriously violent officers of the Ministry for the Promotion of Virtue and the Prevention of Vice (or, informally, the Religious Police) thrashed and jailed men whose beards were too short and women whose burqas showed a little ankle. On the 27th, for 300,000 afghanis (about $5) you could rent a TV, DVD player, and a grab bag of discs of dubious parentage overnight. Television, banned by the eminently uptight Taliban as decadent and foreign, had survived its rule in secret stashes. But now the titles have expanded from such third-world staples as Schwarzenegger's "Commando" and Van Damme's "Universal Soldier" to "Thounders Boobs" (sic), "Climaxic Dyldoos" (sic), and for mujaheddin whose sexual preferences extend beyond or in lieu of their permitted four wives, "Manroot, Twice as Long."

Less than a week after the Taliban fled Taloqan, this TV repair shop was open for business.

"You should see 'Thounders Boobs,'" my 20-year-old translator, Jovid, told me. "It really is quite excellent." No "Manroot" for him.

Certainly any society that fetishizes women by cloistering them even when they're walking down the street—that much certainly hasn't changed, even in the cities—offers a natural market for dirty-movie entrepreneurs. But the post-Taliban sex life of Afghans is transforming more than just their wet dreams.

Many Afghans are doing the unthinkable: They're dating, or to be more specific, fucking without permission. A week and a half ago, the only way you could

Taliban logo being painted over at a school. They waited a week to be sure the Taliban weren't coming back.

get laid here was to get hitched to your parents' friends' child—and you never got to see what was behind door number one until it was too late. People dodged this convention occasionally, but if they got caught by the Religious Police they were offered an uncomfortable choice—being stoned to death or buried alive. "If I want her to come to me, she does," Jovid confided about his girlfriend. Neither of their parents know about this "secret love."

"Do you two have sex?" I asked.

"Of course!" he brightened.

"And if she gets pregnant?"

"In Afghanistan this kind of relationship is just like marriage."

What a difference a few thousand cluster bombs make: Afghanistan has evolved from the Hephthalites and the Sassanids to "Home Fries" in 10 days. And it's not just the kids: Married women are getting busy on the side while their husbands kill their countrymen at the airport. "The important thing," one thirtyish woman said, "is for him not to know about your secret love."

This brought up an intriguing issue. What about prostitution? Not to worry, half a dozen unrelated sources assured me. Men were pimping their daughters to the highest bidder all over town. The going rate: $100 per night. and an impressive variety of ages and ethnicities—Uzbek. Hazara. you name it—were available.

Striking. about a culture condemned by Iran for taking Islam too far. is the fact that few Afghans deign to heed the call to prayer. In neighboring Pakistan, taxi drivers stop their cars in the middle of the street. whip out a prayer mat, and get busy chatting up Allah whenever a nearby loudspeaker belches out a mullah's beseeching cry: here no one even bothers to blink or roll their eyes as they line up at the bustling opium market to score some Friday night rhapsody to go along with a screening of "Thunders Boobs." No one is frying up a meal of pigs' feet wrapped in bacon. at least not yet. but that's more of a concession to regional culinary preferences than strict adherence to Islam.

Even the daytime Ramadan fast. the only aspect of the Muslim religion still universally observed after Taliban logos started getting painted over, fell by the wayside just days later. Countless vendors fired up their grills and began serving up beef and lamb kebabs to eager customers in mid afternoon. "Isn't that illegal?" I asked one such entrepreneur. "People are hungry." he shrugged. "They've been fasting all day."

Even that simplest of Muslim prohibitions. the stricture against drinking alcohol. is yesterday's news. "Please bring wine" is the second line you'll hear after being invited to dinner. The third is: "How about whiskey?" Supplies are sparse. but the way things are going. expect a fully stocked Cork-N-Bottle to open in Kunduz within minutes.

Petty thievery. punishable by amputation until late. has made an impressive comeback in this brave new world of no payback. Throngs of boys blowing off their *madrassa* studies to hang around the Afghan version of the mall bum-rush the slow. the dimwitted, and the foreign. dozens of little hands eagerly snatching watches from wrists and bundles of afghanis from pockets. Gap-toothed graybeards of 40—half the age you'd guess in America —chortle as these children of the corn grab burqaed butts and scamper off to shoplift Iranian sweaters and Chinese lighters.

The ample supply of opium here comes as a real mystery. About a year ago. the Taliban government had announced that Afghanistan. formerly exporter of half the world's heroin. had virtually eradicated its opium crop by the edict of Supreme Leader Mullah Mohammad Omar. The world didn't trust but did verify. and it turned out to be true. No one at the bazaar could explain where the bricks of brown paste had come from so quickly. but they didn't much care: "It is so much cheaper than food." a toothless codger reasoned.

While I talked to him. a fellow journalist arrived with breaking news: Taliban prisoners had tried to escape in Mazar-e-Sharif and were engaging U.S. and British commandos in a ferocious firefight. Secret Talib cells had ambushed Alliance forces in Taloqan and Dasht-e Qal'eh. Northern Afghanistan. it seemed. was once again in play.

"I'd better go home and smoke this while I still can." the old man told me. "I'm glad I didn't shave my beard."

Press conference given by Northern Alliance General Mohammad Daoud in Taloqan. Insert shows Ulf Stromberg, a cameraman for Swedish TV4. Stromberg was murdered in his Taloqan guest house a few days later.

8. Running the Odds
When Nobody Cares

TALOQAN-KOLKUL HWY., AFGHANISTAN, December 3

hey came to kill me. I heard them pounding on my metal door. Everyone in this country who can afford metal doors has them; the sky turns pitch-black and the streets turn ugly at 5 p.m.

The murderers were polite at first. Naturally, I didn't answer the door. It was 3 in the morning and it was Afghanistan. Anyone with a hot lead on an exclusive interview with General Dostum or photos of child mine victims could wait until morning.

Then they pounded angrily. I was glad I hadn't gotten out of my sleeping bag.

They came back at 5, I think it was. They had young voices and they spoke Dari, the *lingua franca* of northeastern Afghanistan and by extension the Northern Alliance. They went away sooner this time.

There were 45 Western journalists living in private homes scattered around Taloqan, a backwater equivalent to a small town in Georgia, which serves as the provincial capital of Takhar Province. Taloqan was just 20 minutes from the front line at Kunduz on a fairly decent road. We were there to cover the siege of Kunduz, the fall of which would also open major roads to Kabul and Mazar-e-Sharif and access to the Uzbek border.

Conditions in the journalists' guest houses were squalid. The better rooms featured a few filthy mats on top of a flea-infested carpet. Heat was furnished by benzene lamps that caused nausea and burning eyes. There was no electricity.

You couldn't eat during the day because it was Ramadan, and you couldn't go out at night. We paid $25 per person per night for these digs. Boiled hot water for bathing was $5 more.

They really got you on food brought in from the bazaar. My favorite price-gouging moment—and there were so many—was my landlord's assertion that eggs were going for a buck each in a country with an average monthly salary of $1.40.

The journalists said that it was all CNN's fault, that the network paid so much for helicopter rides and cool shots of tanks that the Afghans began to believe that all Westerners were made of money. On the other hand, CNN was probably just another victim in a place where taxi drivers think nothing of asking $1,400 for a 10-minute ride.

No one gave a damn about our security. The Northern Alliance never assigned

Khanabad, Afghanistan, east of Kunduz. This area was struck by Taliban shells an hour later. At least one journalist was seriously injured.

guards for our houses or for journalist convoys, which were constantly getting ambushed. And neither the U.S. nor the Alliance would send a chopper for you if you got shot.

The next morning, Nov. 27, I ran into Pedro, a Portugese radio correspondent who lived a few houses away. I asked him if anyone had pounded on his door the night before. "As a matter of fact, yes," he replied.

A few hours later, the news spread that Ulf Stromberg, a 42-year-old Swedish cameraman who'd been living three doors away from me, had answered the door that night to find three or four young men pointing Kalishnikovs at him. When he shouted to alert his roommates, they shot him. The killers robbed the others and fled into the night.

Forty-five journalists had come to Taloqan in my convoy. Stromberg was the third one killed for his money.

I conducted an informal poll of the writers and TV people gathering at the tiny Northern Alliance Foreign Ministry. All had been awakened the night before by knocks at their doors. Only Stromberg had answered. The killers had known where all of us lived. If we had all answered our doors, we all would have been killed for our carefully concealed $100 bills and whatever possessions intrigued them.

"I don't mind dying in battle to get a story," a writer for the French daily *Le Monde* told me. "Getting killed in a stupid street crime is something else altogether."

The Afghans are wrong, of course. We're not loaded. If and when I make it back home, I've got bills piled a foot high to contend with. But they're also right: compared to them, we're zillionaires. One could try a long-term/short-term argument on them—journalists tell the Afghans' story, people back home decide to help out, aid pours in, Afghanistan prospers someday and so do you—but why bother? When the next meal is uncertain, a percentage of the population will act by any means necessary to secure that food and maybe a little extra. The fact that we're taking enormous risks to help them just doesn't matter.

They ripped off Ulf Stromberg again, even after he was dead. Northern Alliance officials initially refused to issue a death certificate or permission to let his body leave the country unless they were paid a $2,000 fee. (This indecent behavior isn't without precedent; another murdered TV man's body was held on the grounds that, like himself, his visa had expired.)

Later that day, Stromberg's colleagues loaded his coffin onto a pickup for the brutal six-hour trip on a bombed-out road to the Tajik border. Both the U.S. and the Alliance refused to send a chopper to spare his corpse this final humiliation.

Finally, at 9 that night, a box containing Stromberg's remains was placed on a tractor-powered barge that crossed the Pyanj River. Next to the coffin rested his backpack and equipment. Covering it was a green tarp covered with the thick, powdery dust of Afghanistan.

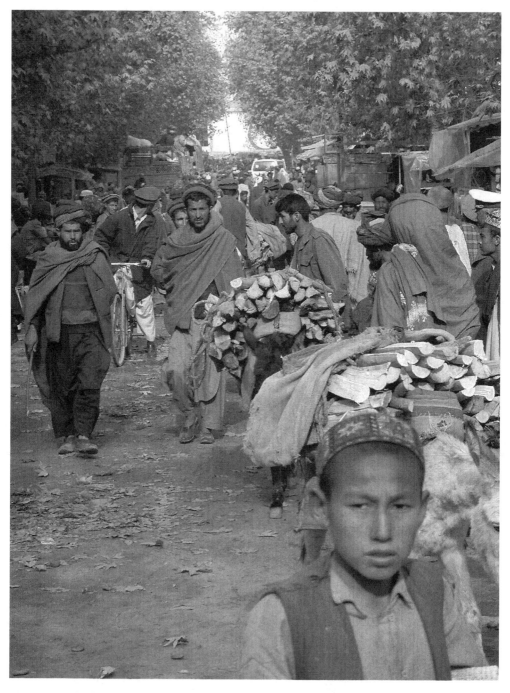

Street scene, Taloqan.

9. Here's to the Middle Ages

Y ou only have to be in this country for a few minutes to understand what an entire presidential administration seated behind faux cherry desks in D.C. hasn't figured out yet: The last thing this country needs is more bombs. Bombing is redundant: death by air strike too pointless to be cruel.

God must have been in a serious funk when He created this geographic leftover between Central and South Asia. Not only did He stick the Afghans with the world's hottest deserts and its coldest mountains. He gave them just two natural resources: rocks and dust. And then, just because He's both ornery and omnipotent, He also gave them neighbors who hate each other so much they won't even touch each other with guns and knives; they let the Afghans do it for them.

"We should nuke this whole country and start from scratch," a New Yorker named David told me over fatty kebabs at the bazaar. And he's a libbie, toiling for a couple of N.G.O. charities here.

Nonetheless, we Americans could learn a lot from the Afghans and their medieval society. Even the most well-traveled visitors here are instantly struck by the way Afghans help one another. To some extent it's self-motivated; helping to push someone's truck out of a ditch gets you moving sooner if it's blocking your way. But the truth is, everyone jumps to the assistance of anyone who needs it without being asked. No one walks by. If you drop a heavy load, a dozen men will rush up and offer not only to assist, but also to carry the item themselves. And no, they're not grabbing your wallet as they do it.

Afghans are rightly famous for their unparalleled skills of subterfuge, dissembling and outright cheating. But things are a lot more complicated than that. Afghans live in a state of perpetual warfare in a land where getting by is tough enough during peacetime. It comes as no surprise that they cut a few corners in the honesty department. What's amazing is how fundamentally decent these people are under such desperate conditions.

As you read this, you're thinking that Americans also help each other in a pinch. But we don't. If we lived like Afghans, you'd stop the instant you saw a broken-down vehicle on the side of the road. So would the car behind you. But you don't stop and neither do I. Afghans don't need an auto club; they have each other.

The tribal system, so detrimental to building an effective multiethnic state, offers tremendous support to people struggling to survive in impossibly difficult times. My translator Jovid's rented adobe-walled box on the outskirts of town here, which would normally house six people, is currently home to 15. Three of them, an old man and his two children, are refugees from nearby Kunduz who walked here after an errant American bomb destroyed their neighborhood. Four more are distant relatives who moved in after four years of drought made farming impossible.

The rest are orphaned children, not even distantly related to Jovid's family. The orphans are from the neighborhood; their mothers starved to death after their fathers died in battle. There are few orphanages in Afghanistan; there's no need for them.

"Someone just takes them in," Jovid replied when I asked him what happens to most orphans. Just to be clear, Jovid's family is desperately poor. Still, it would never occur to them not to feed a hungry person.

After years of reading about a country rigidly divided between a Tajik north and a Pashtun south, in which the Hindu minority was ordered by the Taliban to wear identifying badges—for their own protection, supposedly—I was astonished to discover an altogether different reality. Uzbeks, Daris and Pashtuns not only tolerate one another, they almost all speak each other's languages and partake of various elements of each other's cultures. Tajiks wear Pashtun clothing, Uzbeks eat Turkmen food and Tajiks marry Uzbeks.

While different kinds of Americans live in strictly segregated, monochromatic cities and neighborhoods and can't even stand to hear each other's music, Afghans of all ethnic stripes live side by side in a truly blended nation. This partly explains why yesterday's Taliban can shave, trade his turban for a Nuristani cap, and become Northern Alliance—to jump from a Pashtun- to a Tajik-dominant culture isn't that hard. Afghans make war all the time—it's what they do best—but they fight out of loyalty to a commander or a warlord. They don't shoot each other merely because of the color of their skin. We Americans, who most assuredly know better, do.

And while we've all been treated to vague references to the Afghan tradition of "hospitality to strangers"—mainly to explain the Taliban willingness to eat American lead on behalf of their guest Osama bin Laden—it's something you have to experience personally in order to fully appreciate. To be offered a meal in a home here means that you'll be treated to the equivalent of a Thanksgiving dinner by people who can scarcely afford the minimum caloric intake to get them through the day.

When an emergency arose that required me to go out into the night (Afghans never go out after dark, due to armed rapists and brigands roaming the streets), my hosts insisted that a car and driver be found to take me. Armed to the teeth and willing to risk their lives had I been attacked, they accompanied me to my destination. It was only days later that I inadvertently discovered that they had paid $50—more than a year's salary—for that car.

Crisis, as New Yorkers rediscovered after September 11th, brings people together. If Afghanistan is someday blessed with peace, one hopes that it won't lose the powerful bonds that have kept its people going through the worst that life has to offer.

10. When Life is a Short-term Lease

"How old are you?" the soldier wanted to know. Resplendent in his spiffy new Northern Alliance hat and shiny Pancho Villa ammo belt and matching AK-47, he tiptoed through what some said was a minefield (though he said they were from Badakhshan Province and didn't know Takhar or the mysteries of its mines) to take a leak.

DUSHANBE, TAJIKISTAN, December 7

"Thirty-eight. How about you?"

"How old do you think I am?"

Salt-and-pepper hair, definitely receding. Not just eye bags, but wrinkles. Subtly hard facial angles; not a gram of baby fat. I thought 42. I said 36 to be polite.

He enjoyed a hearty laugh. "I'm 18!"

Middle-aged teen-agers shouldn't come as much of a surprise in a country with an average life expectancy of 43 (considerably less for front-line troops). But when you spend just a few weeks living the same toxic lifestyle as these poor and unlucky souls, it's amazing that they live as long as they do.

All things considered, I lived considerably better than the average resident of Taloqan, Afghanistan, where I just spent a couple of weeks. For one thing, I was willing and able to pay the extortionate rate of five bucks for the sticks you burn to boil bath water in an ancient tin stove. A hot-water *hamam* goes a long way toward improving your outlook after a night spent watching bombs fall far too close to your home address. And call me a spendthrift if you want, but I always sprang for the 60-cent horse-drawn cart ride across town. Most Afghans didn't.

Otherwise, there were few indignities or inconveniences that my Amex, Visa or carefully concealed wad of crisp hundreds could ease, much less eradicate. Like most Afghans, I slept on a filthy mat along one wall of a freezing-cold room containing said stinky mat on top of one astonishingly dirty red carpet. The foul stench made sleep nearly impossible; strange rashes spread among the press corps. Afghans, when asked about this, shrugged and pointed to their own scary blotches.

Though as an infidel I was technically exempt from the 5 a.m.-to-6 p.m. Ramadan fast, the only way to sneak a snack without causing the highly armed locals to take

Taliban POWs at the Taloqan jail. Saw blades serve as window bars. (Photo: Mary Anne Patey.)

offense was to stay home and pay a kid to run to the bazaar. Since I was always out and about, like other journalists I observed a de facto Ramadan fast. Think it's easy? Try it yourself: Move to Arizona and go all day without a sip of water. The principal difference is that Afghanistan is drier and dustier.

Don't get the idea, though, that breaking out that dinnertime flatware after an all-day fast is a big treat. Most people survive on a vegan-unfriendly diet of fatty kebabs and water drawn from the natural goodness of the gutter on the side of the road. When I hungrily inquired about a few plump ducks splashing around in Taloqan's communal bath/drinking fountain/toilet/garbage can, you would have thought I'd said only wimps like AK-47s. "EAT them? Why?" my translator spat in disgust.

"In France," I offered, "ducks are a delicacy."

"Not here," he shuddered. "We need them alive."

"If you don't eat ducks, what good are they?"

"They keep the gutter water clean."

What an atrociously unbalanced and unhygienic diet and American bombs don't finish off, the triple B's—bugs, benzene and breathing—surely will.

For one thing, the nation's bedding supports a thriving ecosystem of fleas, ticks, bed-bugs, lice and other assorted nasties—including everyone's favorite bedtime companion, Mr. Scorpion. Neither warrior nor babe nor Osama himself is safe from the contagion, not to mention painful welts, issued by the local critters. After just one week, I counted 106 bites from Afghan bed fauna, many of them on body parts best left unblemished.

Furthermore, nights are almost always shockingly cold, and so are the days from November through May. Afghans heat their uninsulated mud-adobe homes with Chinese-made camping lanterns fueled by eye-burning, lung-searing benzene. Every teeth-chattering minute offers a terrible dilemma: Which is worse, freezing to death or poisoning yourself on low-grade Central Asian benzene?

Finally, there's the dust. With the consistency of flour, it's kicked up by anything and anyone moving across a 99 percent unpaved landscape. Consequently, everyone in Afghanistan suffers from smoker's cough. I left Afghanistan days ago, yet I'm still ejecting prodigious balls of sandy phlegm.

Perhaps the world will, against all odds, witness the coming of a peaceful, prosperous society in Afghanistan. Maybe Afghans will routinely live well into their 50s. American civilization may bring running water, nay, even clean, fresh Evian, into every home. But who's going to nuke the ferocious fleas I'm bringing home in my luggage?

Rall shopping at the Taloqan bazaar. Huge crowds, unaccustomed to foreigners, followed him everywhere. (Photo: Mary Anne Patey.)

11. A Snake Swallowing A Snake Swallowing Its Tail

NEW YORK, October 23

The terrorists won, and I collaborated with them. And if you've done anything other than deck out your SUV in plastic flags while chanting "YOO-ESS-AY" every time Donald Rumsfeld's smug mug flashes across your screen, you were in on it too.

No one, if the tightlipped Bush Administration is to be believed, has claimed responsibility for the quadruple hijackings and ensuing mayhem of September 11th. But just about everyone agrees that the perps were out to send America some kind of message. Whether that memo reads "quit propping up Israel" or "drop the sanctions against Iraq" or "Muslim fundamentalism is taking over the world so please die and go away" has been debated by every talking head imaginable, but one thing is certain: people fly planes into buildings for a reason.

Suddenly louts who couldn't tell Serbia from Slovenia are fully versed on the Pashtun-Tajik rivalry in Afghanistan, the differences between Sunnis and Shiites and the strategic importance of Mazar-e-Sharif to the Northern Alliance. Recovering ignoramuses who wouldn't have shot a passing glance to a column-inch about the deaths of millions in China are questioning whether State Department policy towards the Arab world may have been so hypocritical and insensitive that it led extremists to get our attention in an incredibly dramatic way.

For the first time in memory, Americans are reconsidering the wisdom of supporting an Israel whose reactions to Palestinian terrorism is itself increasingly indistinguishable from terrorism. We're questioning—not just on the op-ed pages, but in real life—our dependence on foreign oil. We're reevaluating a set of assumptions that has governed American foreign policy since World War II: Isn't it hypocritical for a freedom-loving republic to support repressive dictatorships in Pakistan and Saudi Arabia? Why continue ineffective sanctions that make ordinary Iraqis suffer while Saddam Hussein maintains his luxurious lifestyle?

This new American thoughtfulness, of course, is exactly what the 19 hijackers hoped for during the last few seconds of their lives. Aside from a shot at those newly-famous black-eyed virgins in the post-martyrdom hereafter, they wanted the world's single remaining superpower to stop business as usual in Central Asia and the Middle East. We may be bombing Afghanistan—a tactic that's nothing more than a flashier rehash of Bill Clinton's own Osama fetish—but the days of blindly backing Israel while blindsiding Muslims to get at the oil beneath their sand are *finito*. Terrorism isn't pretty, but it works.

No one wants to cave in to those who massacred thousands of our fellow citizens. But the alternative is even less attractive. If we continue to back every despot willing to run a pipeline through his back yard, his oppressed subjects will invariably strike at the power behind the throne: us. If we refuse to even consider the possibility that our actions abroad are sometimes less than decent and honorable, we can look forward to more such attacks in the future.

On the other hand, even considering—much less meeting—the demands of terrorists invariably leads to more demands. And so the hawks say: Bomb now, think later. Or better yet: just bomb. They have a point, but they're the ones who got us into this mess in the first place.

There is no correct answer to this Escheresque conundrum. Thoughtful reevaluation of American actions throughout the globe, and not just in the Muslim world, is as welcome as it's overdue. Unfortunately, it's also a concession to mass murder. And yet: we obviously can't blunder along as we always have.

Ideally, we Americans and our government would see such events as the bombings of the World Trade Center in 1993, our embassies in Kenya and Tanzania and the *U.S.S. Cole* as signals that we were as clueless as we were unprepared. But there's no rolling back the clock, even under a presidency identical in name, personnel and policy to one from 12 years past. The United States is engaged in a negative-sum game; with victory unachievable, cutting losses will have to suffice. Bringing the guilty to justice while considering the possibility that we may not be perfect doesn't exactly set the American heart pounding, but it'll probably have to do.

From now on, we all have to take sides. So let's conduct a brutal self-examination: which are you, a naive sell-out or an ignorant moron?

Alliance soldiers, Bangi.

12. How We Lost
The Afghan War

W e've lost this war. So how much will it cost?

DASHT-E QAL'EH, AFGHANISTAN, December 6

In 1842, the First Afghan War ended with an infamous retreat across the Hindu Kush that cost between 10,000 and 15,000 Brits and their camp followers their lives. One man, a Dr. William Brydon, survived the Afghans to tell the tale upon his return to a remote outpost of the Raj's Northwest Frontier Province. Eventually a retaliatory expedition returned to slaughter the instigators of their humiliation, but this later victory accomplished nothing. Losing this desolate international leftover inspired testy Sepoys to rise up against their supposed betters, sparking a chain of events that ultimately led to Indian independence, decimated the Empire, and reduced England to a European backwater offering neither steady employment nor edible food to its pasty citizenry.

Ditto for the Russians. After the Great Communist Hope took on the U.S. in a decade-long proxy war between slightly different shades of fanatics, the Soviet Union left half its military equipment, economy, and prestige on the ash heap of history. Blame Gorby and Chernobyl if you want, but the USSR's disintegration into mafia banditry owes more to Stinger-shootin' moojes than Berliners dying to shop on the West Side.

Now a Third Afghan War is wrapping up its final act around Kandahar, and a laughable band of charlatans has lobbied in Bonn, Germany, for the right to rule the unruly. Somehow, if the Bushalopes and the Annanites are to be believed, a New Democratic Afghanistan will be cobbled together from the Hekmatyars and Dostums and Rabbanis, all united under the banner of an 87-year-old king who owes more to Fellini than to Shah Mohammed. And get this: After the Afghan parliament gets together, the burqas will come off, the Wendy's will open up next to the main gate of the Kabul bazaar, and that Internet-famous Unocal pipeline project, dormant for far too long, will begin sucking Kazakh crude out from under the Caspian and into the Pakistani port of Karachi. Next mission: bombing Iraq into capitalism.

The networks aired maps turning from Taliban red to Northern Alliance blue, but here on the ground, as people who prefer to remain anywhere-but like to say, no such thing occurred. Dasht-e Qal'eh and Taloqan and Kunduz all "fell," but 99 percent of the conquerors were Taliban troops who shed their beards and turbans and picked up Shah

Massoud's hip hat for a buck. There were, before September 11, a mere 6,000 to 20,000 Northern Alliance soldiers holding the eastern portion of Takhar province and the extremely mountainous Badakhshan and Wakhan Corridor, an inland peninsula created as a buffer zone between imperial Russia and British India during the 19th century.

When your taxpayer-funded $75,000 bombs began pounding front-line Taliban positions and the not-so-occasional farming village, the age-old Afghan tradition of ideological flexibility and self-preservation led thousands of Taliban to cross the lines to "defect."

"I am so sorry," a Taliban commander cried in the welcoming arms of his Northern Alliance counterpart a day before Kunduz "fell." "We are brothers and should not have fought."

Finally, a rare truth in a land of lies—both men had fought together in the Taliban and before that against the Soviets. The vast majority of "Northern Alliance" fighters now were Taliban a few weeks ago; welcome to the first fashion war of the new millennium.

There are two ways to consider the success of War on Terror, Part One. The first is as an act of retribution against the Taliban for tolerating and supporting Osama bin Laden's Al Qaeda network (never mind that Al Qaeda is bigger and more influential in Pakistan than in Afghanistan or that it is merely one of hundreds of extremist Islamist organizations that trained in Afghanistan). In this view Afghanistan is a source of instability throughout Central Asia and, by extension, for Western oil interests and the West itself. September 11 was merely the latest manifestation of the dangerous extremist phenomenon. Angry Afghans aren't angry at anything America has done, say Rumsfeld and Powell; they're perpetually ornery motherfuckers who have to be kept under lock and key so that the civilized world can get down to the business of the 21st century, which will be one hell of a business if we can ever convince people to stop selling off their mutual funds.

Then there's the liberal, free-market, interventionist approach, which sees the geopolitical collision zone between Central and South Asia as intrinsically doomed by a variety of factors: a strategic location, an absence of natural resources, and far too many guns and mines left over from the '80s. Marshall-Plan the joint, these N.G.O. types say. Build roads, schools, and Virgin Megastores and damn if all of those Uzbeks, Pashtuns, and Tajiks don't simply drop their AKs in favor of Burger King uniforms. And just like that, Americans will be able to shed their fears of 767s cruising through their office towers.

Cooler heads, those who own books by both Rudyard Kipling and Ahmed Rashid, know that Lonely Planet offers the best advice on the best time to visit Afghanistan: "Don't go." But nothing is more certain than this: You can no more control the Afghans than you can help them.

It's a good thing that those snapshots of starving Afghans were taken in refugee camps in Quetta; you have to work hard to find hunger here. That's good too, since Afghans aren't getting any of that much vaunted food aid, unless they pay top afghani

107

Coffin of slain cameraman Ulf Stromberg leaves Afghanistan via Pyanj River barge to Tajikistan. (Photo: Mary Anne Patey.)

for it at the market.

Feed starving people out of bags covered with your flag and they'll love you, the theory goes. But based on this precept, no one in Afghanistan has any cause to even *like* you.

Even our military contribution isn't earning the U.S. any I.O.U.s. "We appreciate the bombs you dropped on the Taliban," a veteran Alliance commander named Amin (many Afghans use only one name) told me. "But you bombed airports and roads that we need to run the country. And my men are dying because they have old Russian weapons and you Americans won't fully support us."

What do you want from America?

"Go home and leave us alone."

The principal goal of this adventure in imperialistic vengeance, it seems obvious, should be to install a friendly government in Kabul. But we're winning neither hearts nor minds among either the commoners or the leadership of the current regime apparent.

"How can you talk of imposing that old king on us?" Amin snaps. "Even my father doesn't remember who he is."

A bolder nation-building objective, to reshape medieval Afghanistan from a land of donkeys lugging bundles of sticks into something resembling modernity—i.e., us—has actually moved further away since the beginning of the bombing. Along with the demise of Talibanism's more unusual strictures against kites, pigeons, and women, has come a reversion to the pre-nation-state feudalism that prevailed the last time this regime ran things, from 1992 to 1996.

When a Swedish cameraman was murdered in a Taloqan push-in robbery, journalists asked their liaison at Foreign Ministry to advise them as to which authorities would handle the investigation. "There will be no investigation," came the perfunctory reply.

"But a crime has been committed," a Portuguese television editor insisted. "Where do Afghans go to report crimes?"

"They go home. Nowhere."

The system of governance espoused by anarchokids on St. Marks Place is in full effect here beyond Thunderdome. "You can kill anyone you want, provided they don't have any friends," my translator Jovid assured me. "Nothing will happen."

Thus it's no surprise that Afghanistan has become a gangland paradise. Sign up for service with a local warlord and see the world. You'll die young whether or not you join, but at least your friends will kill your killer if you do.

Americans, mostly of the right and the post-9-11 squishy left, want Afghanistan and its jihad boys out of their hair. For the most part, the barn door has long remained open—tens of thousands of jihad grads are everywhere from Alabama to Alberta, and camps remain operational in Pakistan, Tajikistan, Kyrgyzstan, and elsewhere. But even assuming that the locals are mistaken about Osama having packed up for a new cave on the Pakistani side of the Kashmiri Line of Control, closing the Taliban Club isn't likely to put an end to Islamic extremism here. For one thing, the Northern Alliance itself remains a hotbed of Muslim fundamentalism—with few exceptions, women remain out of sight and out of work. Sharia law still enforces stoning as punishment ("but we will use only small stones," Judge Ahamat Ullha Zarif notes), and America is still viewed as a blank-check endorser of Israeli war crimes and Saudi corruption. And for all of America's talk of dropping as many yellow food packs—I haven't seen a single one, by the way—as bombs, Bush Deux is already losing interest in this accursed buffer state just as his father did after the Soviet withdrawal in 1989.

"Next target: Saddam," reads a handwritten sign on a derelict Soviet tank outside a "secret" American base south of the Uzbek border. "It would take billions of dollars to even begin rebuilding this country," an American officer who refused to give his name noted while his driver worked on a flat tire. "Billions of dollars and many, many years. We don't have that kind of attention span. Bombing Iraq will be a lot sexier than teaching Afghans how to read."

And so we've lost this war, not because they're good or we're not, but because of who we are. The American Empire can't spend the bodies or the time or the cash to fix this crazyass place, because in the final analysis, election-year W. was right—we're not nation builders. Guys who once called themselves Talibs switch to something called the Northern Alliance, and we call this a victory. We know it isn't so, but like Nixon's peace with honor, it'll have to do.

Both the Russians and the English lost everything to Afghanistan, but it doesn't have to end that way for us. After all, the same thing happened to us in Vietnam, our first Afghanistan, but we survived it. True, our economy was never the same. Undeniably, it replaced an American Century with postmodern alienation and ironic detachment. But if estimates are correct, if this war is costing a mere billion bucks a month, we ought to tally up our dead, write off our losses, and count ourselves lucky to still be considered a superpower. The British, no slouches in the empire-building business, invaded and occupied Afghanistan three times; the Soviets, pretty damned good at world domination themselves, had their chance. Both lost everything. Why does George W. Bush think he'll succeed where Queen Victoria and Leonid Brezhnev failed?

Epilogue

NEW YORK, May 3, 2003

T he release of *To Afghanistan and Back* in paperback format gave me an unexpected opportunity to take a look back on the year since it first came out and examine it in light of subsequent events. At this juncture, I feel confident that the book, and my reasons for going to Afghanistan in the first place, still hold up.

I went to Afghanistan in November and December 2001 in order to cover the war for The Village Voice and KFI radio. The idea of writing this book came later. *To Afghanistan and Back* was the brainchild of my publisher, Terry Nantier. Terry thought that a cartoon rendition of my experiences covering the invasion could make a good graphic novel in the tradition of cartoonist-war correspondent Joe Sacco. (Sacco has written highly acclaimed graphic novels about the conflicts in Yugoslavia and Palestine.) We both hoped, given my unconventional take on things, that *Afghanistan* might also serve as a counterbalance to the mindless jingoism then being pumped out by major American newspapers and television networks.

Given a choice between spending a year or more working on a project that might be distributed to an indifferent public — would anyone care about the Afghan war once the U.S. had attacked Iraq and/or North Korea? — or rushing to get it out in a timely manner, I decided to go along with my publisher's instincts to produce an "instant" graphic novel. We went to press in February 2002 for a book that appeared in bookstores two months later. The innate problems created by a tight deadline — *Afghanistan* was designed, written and drawn in a breathless six weeks — proved a perverse challenge...like going to Afghanistan in the first place, I suppose.

It was a stupid thing to do, and I don't regret it.

One of my many character flaws is small-C conservatism: I prefer not to form, much less express, strong opinions about events before the dust fully settles. And while I hold lukewarm views about a lot of issues, I doubt that anyone finds milquetoast punditry any more engaging than I do. So I usually keep my moderate views to myself.

My post-9/11 commentaries about the Bush Administration's exploitation of 3,000 murdered office workers to promote a radically partisan political agenda ultimately

111

became famous or infamous — depending where you stand on these things — for their stridency and unwillingness to assume a more deferential tone to those in power. But I got off to a slow start: I was one of the few political cartoonists not to draw anything at all on September 11, 2001.

It was a decision made in cognizance of my jittery mental state. I was freaked out, a couple of Ground Zero refugees were crashing on my futon, and nobody really knew what was going on — who had carried out the attacks, whether more suicide bombings were imminent, whether any survivors would emerge from the rubble six miles south of my Manhattan apartment, how much asbestos was in the air. What could I say? I was tired and sad and shocked and surprised and confused. So what? No one should care how Ted Rall felt about 9/11, especially when Ted Rall felt pretty much the same as everyone else. As my mom says: When in doubt, never miss a chance to shut up.

In the end, waiting a few days before picking up my pen served me well. My colleagues at the big dailies, pressed by anxious editors for an instantaneous reaction to that Tuesday's events, cranked out nearly a hundred virtually identical, identically idiotic renditions of the Statue of Liberty weeping under a cloud of smoke. I might have committed similar crimes against taste and originality had I spoken to the world before having anything intelligent to say.

Books require considerably more consideration than a single cartoon. My previous works analyzed events with the cold-blooded benefit of substantial hindsight: *Revenge of the Latchkey Kids* gave my father a working over for transgressions that predated the first *Star Wars* (which, incidentally, he took me to see on opening day) and *My War With Brian* dealt with my years in junior high school. Afghanistan had been an exhausting, brutalizing, depressing and infuriating experience. I was ashamed of my country for allowing its leaders to carry out awesome brutality against innocent people. I couldn't get the visuals out of my head. Bodies. Chunks of flesh. Blood. When someone suffers a mortal injury, there's more, and less, blood than you'd think.

When I asked Afghans of every ethnic stripe why they thought the Americans were bombing their country, their answer was invariably the same: garden-variety imperialism. The British had invaded Afghanistan when they ruled the world; the Russians had invaded when they ruled Asia. Now the Americans ran everything — and it was their turn to inflict more misery, more war, on the Afghans. September 11th? They couldn't fathom the event, much less see 9/11 as a pretext for war. Few buildings in Afghanistan are taller than two stories — how could people wrap their minds around two towers, each 110 floors high, where 60,000 people worked? And Al Qaeda, everyone knew, was in Pakistan.

Some of my smartest and best-read friends had casually swallowed the official Bush Administration line about the war. Afghan women had been liberated. Thanks to precision bombing, only a few civilians — collateral damage, ick — had gotten killed. We had dropped bright-yellow pre-packaged pasta packages along with the bombs. With the Taliban gone, American troops patrolling the streets and aid agencies passing out food, everything was going to turn out just peachy.

I explained that women were still wearing *burqas*, that Sharia law (radical Islamic strictures that support the stoning of adulterers and thieves being amputated in soccer stadiums) remained in full force, that U.S. peacekeeping troops were only patrolling Kabul — the one city that didn't need them. I told them that the nights belonged to gangs of roving bandits, that gunfire and the screams of rape victims filled the streets, that American warplanes bombed cities that belonged to the Northern Alliance, that our pilots blew up carloads of civilians just for fun. I tried to explain how a 15,000-pound daisy cutter dropped on a bridge in Kunduz might hit its target with impeccable accuracy as it took out the surrounding neighborhood. Invariably they'd give me that quizzical "what? no Santa Claus?" look. "But I saw it on CNN," they'd say, "girls were going back to school. And didn't some chick burn her *burqa*?" What could I tell them — that they hadn't seen what they had seen with their own eyes? They hadn't, of course. But nothing is more maddening than the knowledge of an uncomfortable, hard-to-come-by truth. If you ever get kidnapped by a UFO, shut up. Keeping it to yourself might drive you nuts, but The Look will make you lose it altogether.

Oh, and no one I met saw any yellow pasta packs.

This was my mindset as I sorted through fonts and cover colors. I had six weeks to put together some mélange of cartooning and prose in a readable format that expressed the story I wanted to tell. When the going gets tough, the smart take shortcuts: Rather than crank out the lengthy, carefully researched analysis of the motivations behind the American invasion and its effect on the people and politics of Afghanistan and Central Asia that I would have preferred, I took a cue from Bill Mauldin's World War II classic *Up Front* by reprinting dispatches that I had filed from the front. These bookend what NBM and I came to call the "graphic novella." (Full-length graphic novels like *Brian* and my

113

Rall writing a story in his Taloqan guest house. (Photo: Mary Anne Patey.)

Orwell parody *2024* are closer to a hundred pages.)

Rereading some of my dispatches from Afghanistan now make my toes curl, and not in a good way. I recognize in them a version of myself who hadn't eaten or slept in days, a guy who had difficulty typing from fear or the cold or both, and who as a consequence couldn't muster the clever turns of phrase which allow me to fool myself into believing that I'm a fairly decent writer. I went entire days without eating or taking a leak. I was often thinking about creature comforts while I was trying to write. Authenticity comes at a price, you know?

Still, I think it works. I've read everything I could get my hands on about the Afghan war since I turned in this book, much of it quite good, but nothing else makes me *feel* what it was *like*. Book reviewers — even the negative ones — seem to agree. If you're looking for a military history or analysis of rising Islamic fundamentalism in South Asia, you should probably start elsewhere. But if you want to feel the itch of fresh flea bites, the acrid orange aftertaste of ancient Ashi-Mashi cola and the thud of the bombs across town, you've come to the right place.

I drew the graphic novella while a million random memories and emotions swirled in my head, but whatever confusion spilled out of my Rapidograph pens onto those 50 pages was mitigated by wallowing in the freshness of the details. I drew mountains based on photos I'd taken weeks earlier. The dust I'd choked on seemed easier to draw when it was still coming out of my clothes in the wash. Here too I took a shortcut: rather than analyze a war that was, and is, ongoing, I used the graphic novella to give readers a "Kunduz falls to the Northern Alliance, and YOU ARE THERE" quality. For better or for worse, the art section is about being a journalist, covering the war, and — did I mention? — being scared shitless. Lots of artists could have drawn it more accurately, perhaps. But that's how it felt to me. Still.

A question comes up often: wasn't I scared? Several listeners to my satellite uplinks on Los Angeles' KFI radio remarked on my shaky voice one night when the bombs were falling particularly fast and thick. It was freezing and I *was* jittery. To tell the truth, I was terrified from the moment I first set foot on the Afghan side of the Pyanj River until the happy vision of my Tajik fixer waving his arms at me from the Soviet-built dock three weeks later. I was less frightened at some points than at others, but I was never *not* scared. We slept with our boots on. I planned out an escape route over the back wall of my guest house. I slept like a cat, with one eye open, in case I needed to grab my emergency sack containing money, my passport, a satellite phone and silk underwear. Every sound made me jump. And everyone had big guns.

"It is true. You will see," Carmen, a Moscow-based correspondent for Portuguese radio who'd been rotated through Afghanistan a month earlier, had told me in Taloqan.

A roadside cemetery, Taloqan.

"You will cry with joy to see Dushanbe again. You will dream of the breakfast buffet at the Hotel Tajikistan." Dushanbe is a dump and the Hotel Tajikistan is a horror, but she was right. I've never felt sorrier for anybody than the busload of illegal immigrants I witnessed being deported back to Afghanistan by the Tajiks.

Every moment you spend in Afghanistan may be your last. Name your poison: there are countless reasons that few Afghans make it past forty years of age. You might, for example, trip a mine when you go to urinate. A boy living a few blocks down the street from my place took his last whizz that way; I heard that he lasted a couple of hours and died without learning that his legs were gone. That may have been for the best.

A guy might walk up to you in the street and pop you with an AK; alternatively rounds aimed at someone else might take you out as you head to the neighborhood kebob stand. Powering up a satellite phone turned one into a target for Taliban mortars and American missiles — national loyalties count for nothing when a Predator drone plane zeroes in on you, guided by some clown with an iMac in Bethesda. Strolling around town as an unarmed journalist carrying thousands of dollars in cash, with no police force or clan affiliation to protect you, ups the ante. At least Afghans are comforted by the knowledge that their murder will be avenged by the killings of their assassin as well as everyone who has ever met him. Add malnutrition, filthy water and ancient pestilences to a situation in which medical care is virtually nonexistent, and it feels like the country itself is out to get you. Afghanistan is a prescription for an early grave under a mound of rocks topped by a stick holding a tattered white cloth, and that's the status of most Afghans.

Not all the war correspondents were nervous. My wife asked a journalist covering the Khanabad front why he didn't wear a bulletproof vest. (At $1,200 each, we couldn't afford them.) "Are you kidding?" the heavyset photographer for *The San Jose Mercury News* replied as he wiped his brow. "It's too hot out here." A writer for another big daily shrugged off a band of weird welts on her waist and lower back. Everyone agreed that it was probably Lyme's disease, a common hazard spread by Afghanistan's ferocious fleas. "I'll live," she said. Five days earlier, she'd ridden into town on an armored personnel carrier with Taliban bullets all around. She wasn't going to let a bug get her down.

Then again, reporters for the big dailies and television networks faced fewer risks than those who traveled independently. If they got robbed, a call on a satellite phone would dispatch a courier with a fat bundle of crisp hundreds across the Pyanj. "Did you hear if someone brought in my $5,000?" a writer for *The Washington Post* asked me when I drove into town. In a war zone, money solves most problems. If an Afghan war journo got shot, his employer might be able to charter a Northern Alliance chopper to spirit him out to Tajikistan. NBC spent thousands to run Alliance helicopters in and out of Kabul: their staff refused to file reports and to deliver the goods without a steady supply of Russian beer.

On the other hand, independent reporters and those who worked for smaller outfits couldn't get any more cash if they needed it — and those who could inflated prices for those who couldn't. We small fry lived on the edge. Anything that went wrong was fatal. If I had died, I would probably have been buried in Afghanistan. In all seriousness, there wouldn't have been enough money to bribe the local warlord into releasing my corpse for export.

Why didn't the mainstream media corroborate my reports? The European media did. British newspapers like *The Guardian* and *The Independent* and broadcast outlets like the BBC filed truthful, accurate reports from the front. They reported what actually happened: American attempts to fight on the cheap and occupy the country with insufficient personnel, extensive civilian casualties, cozying up to the very warlords we should have been killing along with the Taliban, the Bush Administration's sleazy maneuvering to revive Unocal's old gas pipeline project from Turkmenistan to Pakistan via Afghanistan. (I later wrote about this in a book called *Gas War: The Truth Behind the American Occupation of Afghanistan.*) The United States' great accomplishments in Afghanistan were to replace the world's worst regime with lawlessness and anarchy, and to increase contempt for Americans among Muslims who already thought we were scum. All of the details were available to anyone who cared to get their news from foreign sources, all readily available on the internet — but that's not how most people get their news.

Americans counted on American reporters and news services to report and explain the war. Mostly, they watched the evening news and read the morning paper. With few exceptions, most coverage from Afghanistan was blatantly inaccurate, laughably biased or both. Almost all of it suffered from mortal sins of omission.

Only one of the major networks dispatched a full camera crew to northern Afghanistan, where the last major fighting of the war took place. Those reporters moved into Mohammad Daoud's heavily fortified personal compound near the soccer field-helicopter landing pad-execution ground in the center of town. General Daoud, the Northern Alliance's warlord in Takhar province, provided his guests with the only reliable electricity in Taloqan, lavish spreads of sumptuous food and, most crucially, a battalion of young men armed to the teeth to ensure that they didn't meet the fate of Ulf Stromberg. (Stromberg, like me, lived with an ordinary Afghan family, in the 'hood.) They knew what Daoud wanted them to know and went where he took them, surrounded by their personal army of rented bodyguards. They never hung out, as I did, in the bazaars to talk to the locals. They never met with Taliban prisoners or leaders. They never knew that the roads were full of refugees from American bombs or that Talibs still controlled part of the city. They covered what was essentially a civil war while *living with one side of the conflict*. And they paid a leader of that side tens of thousands of dollars to stay safe and warm.

Was I envious? Hell, yes. During Ramadan, food was only available at night — when it was unsafe to go outside. I went hungry. I am now convinced that humans can subsist indefinitely on a reliable stash of Qatari Pepsi in rusty cans. Nevertheless, I would have refused General Daoud's hospitality had it been offered. Those ersatz journalists were guilty of a serious ethical lapse. They chose sides. They traded truth for access, and disseminated lies to their viewers. What they gave the folks back home was bullshit: you can't tell the world about Northern Alliance atrocities when you rely on them for your safety and comfort. Needless to say, they never reported their conflict of interest or

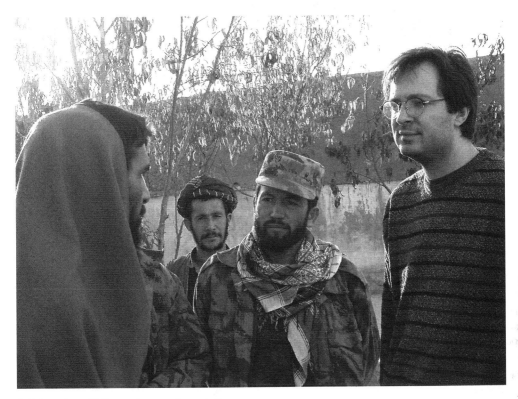

Rall interviews Taliban prisoner of war, left.

revealed that they had subjected themselves to voluntary self-censorship.

Many journalists, particularly the TV people, didn't settle for merely covering the action. On slow days, they bought news.

Sometimes there was no fighting on the front. As any veteran will tell you, war is a lot of sitting around doing nothing punctuated by occasional bursts of wild, chaotic panic. But the viewers back home in the States didn't want to see a lot of dudes hanging around talking. So the TV guys would pay Northern Alliance commanders $250 a shell to fire rounds at an empty field. They hitched rides — at the bargain rate of $2,000 a person — inside tanks and APCs. (A few of the foreign journalists killed in Afghanistan died when "their" tanks wandered into a Taliban ambush.) It's the first commandment of journalism: cover the news, don't *become* the news. But American TV reporters paid for mortars, photographs of casualties, even for the battles themselves.

American audiences wanted to see Afghan liberation, and so they did. Camera crews wandered city streets offering $200 to any woman willing to shed her *burqa* for the folks back home. The women, many of them widowed by war and reduced to abject poverty by Taliban prohibitions against working, balanced the anger of their male neighbors against the hunger of their children. Some of them, fewer than you'd guess, lifted their veils and smiled for a million television sets around the globe. When the scene was finished, the *burqa* went right back on. You see, the average Afghan earns about four dol-

119

lars per month.

Girls went back to school — that much is true. They were the same girls, from relatively well-off families, who had gone to school during Taliban rule. Although their treatment of women was appalling in numerous respects, the Taliban had never officially banned female students. In most of Afghanistan, anyone who can afford the $12 cost of a school uniform and whose parents can kick in to pay a teacher can go to class. Few girls, or boys for that matter, met those requirements either before or after the installation of the Northern Alliance government. If more boys than girls received a formal education in Afghanistan, it was because their parents made that choice. Afghanistan's culture is deeply patriarchal. American journalists preferred to present a black-and-white image of liberated girls to such fuzzy political realities.

Did seeing those Afghan schoolgirls make you feel better? Good. It was supposed to.

Few Americans are aware that the hand-picked puppet president, Hamid Karzai, rules only Kabul and its immediate suburbs. Ishmael Khan, the violent self-proclaimed emir of Herat, runs a singularly organized — traffic signals, electricity, cops — fiefdom along the northwestern frontier with Iran. Uzbek warlord Rashid Dostum, accused of complicity in the massacre of thousands of Taliban prisoners after the events discussed in this book, controls Kunduz province and the strategically-important city of Mazar-e-Sharif. Gul Agha Sherzai owns Kandahar, and Mullah Mohammad Omar is working to reconstitute his Taliban militia from his base in southern Helmand province. U.S. newspapers call these places "outlying areas" or "the provinces." Yet the current situation since the U.S. invasion is comparable to establishing law and order only in Washington while leaving "outlying areas" like Los Angeles and Chicago — the whole country — to rapists, robbers and murderers. Would that be liberation? A few thousand American troops are stationed in a solitary cantonment at the former Soviet air base at Bagram near Kabul, and that's it — the vast majority of Afghanistan's population has been thrown to the wolves.

On January 2, 2003 *The New York Times* reported that even in Kabul — the only place governed by Karzai — not one house has thus far been built with international assistance. According to the United Nations, 650,000 Kabuli refugees urged by the U.S. to return home to Afghanistan remain homeless. Millions of Afghans in "outlying provinces" are without shelter. Few have received food or housing. British troops were forced to dip into their own pockets to buy a generator to heat Kabul's Indira Gandhi hospital. If the U.S. has plans to rebuild Afghan roads, install a telephone system or otherwise create a viable infrastructure, it has yet to announce them.

Although the quality of life for the average Afghan has continued to deteriorate, this was the dismal state of affairs in January 2002, when CBS News and *The New York Times* asked Americans what they thought of their war. Afghanistan was an unmitigated disaster. Osama bin Laden escaped, opium cultivation made its comeback and the United States made more enemies among Muslims around the world. Yet 87 percent of respondents approved of the military attacks against Afghanistan. Only nine percent thought the war had gone badly. Unlike the members of the network TV crew who lived with a warlord and ate his food and accepted his protection, one can't blame the American people for their ignorance. They only know what they're allowed to see.

It's what they leave out

I am frequently asked about the mechanics of media censorship, or more frequently self-censorship, in the United States. I believe that the issue isn't so much a matter of outright lying — though that happens — as one of simply leaving things out to ensure continued access to powerful politicians and other leaders they consider to be potential sources of news.

One of the most striking aspects of life in Third World countries is information starvation. Because they've learned not to trust their state-controlled media, people in authoritarian backwaters carefully debrief newcomers. What's going on abroad? What's going on here? Did you get any foreign newspapers or magazines through customs?

News is a component of infrastructure every bit as important as roads and telephones. Businesspeople need to know if a border with a neighboring country is open so they can decide whether or not to send out a truck. Citizens need to know their government's international standing—are those falling bombs their leader's fault? Hunger for news hurts a country almost as much as hunger for food.

The First Amendment enshrines freedom of the press in the U.S. Constitution, but a variety of forces conspire to prevent totally free access to information. Residents of most cities rely on one large daily newspaper, usually part of a media conglomerate that itself owns the biggest local radio and television stations. Directors of that corporation and the editors who work for them are frequently loathe to offend influential government officials and business tycoons, for if they get cut off — excluded from access to press releases, interviews, leaks, etc. — their ability to collect news is impeded. One might argue that such "news" is little more than worthless propaganda, but fear of causing offense often inhibits the media's natural role as a watchdog of democracy.

Our government very rarely censors the media. It doesn't have to.

A new, subtle form of self-censorship has recently become commonplace. A news story is covered in full, minus a crucial fact that changes the entire tenor of the piece. That missing bit of information is invariably something that would make someone important look bad.

The American media has, for example, devoted extensive coverage to political unrest in Venezuela, where mobs loyal to President Hugo Chávez clashed with striking employees of the state oil company. The crisis sparked an attempted coup d'état in April 2002. To busy Americans, this looks like a simple story of a right-wing Latin American dictator crushing poor workers. That's because three key facts were regularly omitted from the story. First, the oil company strike was called by its wealthy managers, not its workers. Second, Chávez was democratically-elected. Third, the coup plotters were backed by the Bush Administration. "We were sending informal, subtle signals that we don't like this guy," said a U.S. Defense Department official quoted in *The Guardian*, an English paper that has become an important post-9/11 resource for Americans in search of objective reporting. The bully, it turns out, is us — not Chávez, who is standing up for his nation's poor.

Similarly, the North Korean crisis looks like a simple case of crafty commies welching on their agreement not to develop nukes in exchange for economic aid. Repeatedly left out of the thousands of words spilled daily on this topic are the contents of the 1994 North Korea-U.S. Agreed Framework, in which President Clinton promised to develop full diplomatic relations with Kim Jung Il's regime, and North Korean warnings dating to 1999 that they would resume nuclear research unless the U.S. kept up its end of the bargain.

North Korea is violating the agreement. But the U.S. broke it years earlier.

The closest thing to a "smoking gun" found on weapons of mass destruction by U.N. arms inspectors in Iraq was 12 warheads found at an ammo dump south of Baghdad. Americans know that the White House considered this discovery a "material breach" that justified war. Few are aware that, as reported January 17, 2003 in the *U.K. Telegraph*, the canisters were empty, and are probably American-made shells sold to Iraq by the Reagan administration. Not much of a "smoking gun."

Scratch the surface and you find this sort of thing all over the "news." Democratic complaints that proposed Bush tax cuts only benefit the "richest one percent" of Americans are duly reported, but leave out a definition of the term. Did you know that you have to earn more than $330,000 a year to be in the top one percent? Nineteen percent of Americans don't. They told Time that they think they're in that top one percent.

Perhaps you've read that American soldiers are fighting off guerrillas loyal to warlord Gulbuddin Hekmatyar in eastern Afghanistan. Hekmatyar, the Associated Press says, is "believed by Afghan and U.S. authorities to be allied with Taliban and Al Qaeda remnants." That may be true. But Hekmatyar was always a sworn enemy of the Taliban — until the CIA tried to kill him in May 2002, with a Hellfire missile fired by a Predator drone plane.

One missing detail. Changes the story a little, doesn't it?

Debunking the debunkers

A new phenomenon surfaced in the months after 9/11: the right-wing "debunker." This new breed of self-appointed political police scanned the nation's newspapers and airwaves in search of those who dared oppose Bush, his policy of preemptive wars and his domestic programs. Ironically but unsurprisingly, most of the debunkers ended up proving themselves spinmasters of the lowest order. This is my reply to one such writer, who took issue with my assertion that access to Caspian Sea energy resources was an important motivation for the war on terrorism and the U.S. invasion of Afghanistan.

Writing for the website SpinSanity on October 15, 2001, Bush apologist Brendan Nyhan ridiculed my "absurd suggestion that the war [in Afghanistan] is 'solely' about an oil deal, trivializing the overriding motive of the attacks — going after Osama bin Laden's terrorist network and the regime that harbors bin Laden."

Nyhan's widely-circulated hit piece, commissioned by one of those outfits run by liberals so anxious to seem "non-partisan" that they mostly bash liberals (beware the man who says he's fair), was one among a volley of attacks that rained down on progressive commentators who dared to whisper three painfully obvious truths:

First, even before the 9/11 attacks, the well-oiled Bush Administration (bad pun intended) planned to take over Afghanistan one way or another. The only question was how and when it would be carried out.

American-aligned Kazakhstan sits atop the largest untapped oil reserves on earth, but can currently get its crude only as far south as Turkmenistan. Karachi, Pakistan's port on the Indian Ocean, awaits American oil tankers. Between lies Afghanistan; thus Unocal Corporation's $1.9 billion plan to run an 870-mile pipeline to link the Turkmen oil refinery at Charjou to Karachi. Trying to unify fractured Afghanistan under a regime (any regime) that would ensure the safety of a U.S.-sponsored pipeline, President Clinton funded the Taliban from the origins in 1995 until their "guest" Osama bin Laden bombed two American embassies in east Africa in 1998. The Unocal plan was shelved until September 11th gave Bush the pretext he needed to begin bombing and regain momentum for the pipeline plan.

Second, the ersatz "war on terror" has little to do with reducing, much less preventing, terrorist acts by Islamic extremists. The CIA has itself to blame for funding and arming these "evil doers" in the first place; the advantage of creating your own enemies is that you get to know them well in the process. Had the Third Afghan War actually been motivated by vengeance. Rumsfeld & Co. would have targeted groups in the countries that carried out the 9/11 attacks — Saudi Arabia. Egypt and Pakistan. Had it been pro- phylactic. the DOD would have bombed the biggest guerrilla training camps. which were, and still are. in Pakistan. And if the State Department had wanted to deny extrem- ist groups the vast majority of their funding — millions of tiny donations collected in mosques throughout the Arab world — it would have denied them their most potent and legitimate rallying cry: unlimited U.S. support for Israel's home-grown terrorist Ariel Sharon.

Ninety-nine percent of the estimated 5.000 to 15.000 Afghans killed by U.S. bombs had absolutely nothing to do with 9/11. That's an atrocity. it's even worse than 9/11 and Arabs know it. Thanks to George W. Bush. you and I are now significantly more likely to die in an attack by Islamists. Remember: to the rest of the world. we are terrorists.

Third. Nyhan takes me to task for "the insinuation that U.S. policymakers don't care about the victims of the September 11th terrorist attacks or the oppressed women of Afghanistan." Insinuation. hell. I'll say it loud and clear. Let's take the last part first. The Taliban ruled Afghanistan from 1996 to 2001. more than half that time with direct or indirect American financing. Yeah. you say. but that was under Clinton. And yet. for the first seven and a half months of his presidency. Bush never issued a single statement crit- icizing the Taliban's treatment of women. During that period. he found numerous oppor- tunities to discuss tax cuts. fast-track signing authority on free trade and countless other inanities. Long-suffering Afghans. it seems. only matter to U.S. policymakers insofar as they affect The Great Pipeline Project.

What about the 9/11 victims? Well. it was the Bushies who rushed through legisla- tion depriving survivors of their right to sue the government or the airlines. When push came to shove. Bush sold out the victims for a few millionaire airline CEOs. Let's all repeat it together: the victims. American and Afghan. have been used by this vile. cyni- cal administration to line the pockets of its corporate sponsors. And now our soldiers are dying. not for nothing. but while carrying out orders that are making things even worse.

Dying for nothing would be an improvement.

Nyhan and other Bush aficionados' "debunk" the idea of a link between the Afghan war and the pipeline scheme using a line of reasoning lifted from "The Simpsons": We bombed Afghanistan because of 9/11. not oil. "Oil may be a factor." allows Nyhan. but it is a sideshow: the main event is bagging Osama.

Um. but the Taliban offered to turn him over and we turned them down. And we still haven't found him. And Bush now says it was never about bagging Osama.

The fact is. it's mostly about oil. 9/11 or no 9/11, the U.S. would never have invad- ed Afghanistan minus its oil component. Don't we deserve 75-cent-a-gallon gas in return for losing four planes and two big buildings?

As Homer replies when Marge asks him if he's lost his faith in God: "Nooooo! Noooo! No. No. No. No. Well. yes."

I expected the Bushies to wait a decent interval to prove me right about their real motivations in Afghanistan. but the President's high approval ratings must have gone to their heads.

Unocal-related discussions began while the bombs were still falling last October and

125

picked up steam after Bush appointed an ex-Unocal consultant, Zalmay Khalilzad, as his special envoy to Afghanistan.

Then, on March 7, 2002, Afghan interim prime minister Hamid Karzai (yet another former Unocal employee) flew to Ashkhabat to meet with Turkmen president-for-life Saparmurat Niyazov. "There is a project from Turkmenistan, over Afghanistan to Pakistan and then India. We agreed to discuss this soon, both together and with the leader of Pakistan," summarized Niyazov. "Everyone would benefit. Afghanistan would receive employment and a twelfth of the overall profits."

The Pakistani piece of the revived pipeline project (which will likely be built by — surprise! — Unocal) clicked into place February 8, 2002 when Karzai met with military dictator Pervez Musharraf in Islamabad.

But what of Bush's self-avowed pledges to help the oppressed people of Afghanistan live in peace and dignity? Though our soldiers will remain "indefinitely," according to the Associated Press on March 28, 2002, "the Bush administration says it will not send American peacekeepers to the country." In other words, U.S. troops are there not to help the Afghan people, but to train Karzai's puppet army so they can eventually protect American business interests?

Nooooo! No! No. No. No. Well, yes.

Recommended Reading

Ahmed Rashid's **Taliban: Militant Islam, Oil and Fundamentalism** (Yale University Press, 2000) is the definitive work about Afghanistan and the relationship between the Taliban, the U.S. and Pakistan during the late '90s. For further insight about the region, check out his **The Resurgence of Central Asia: Islam or Nationalism?** (Oxford University Press, 1994). Rashid's **Jihad: The Rise of Militant Islam in Central Asia** (Yale University Press, 2002) focuses on the former Soviet Central Asian republics but is nonetheless essential for those interested in Afghanistan's regional influence.

Peter Hopkirk's **The Great Game: The Struggle for Empire in Central Asia** (Kodansha America, 1994) is an entertaining look at 19th century superpower politics between Great Britain and Russia. "The Great Game," as Kipling called it, now focuses on a rivalry between the U.S. and Russia.

Though difficult to find, the Swiss-published **Essential Field Guide to Afghanistan** (Crosslines Communications, 1998) is the only serious English-language travel book currently in print about the country.

The **Central Asia Phrasebook** (Lonely Planet, 1998) covers the major languages of the region. The book's Pashto section is useful in Afghanistan; although it omits Dari, the *lingua franca* of the Northern Alliance, Tajik is included.

About
Ted Rall

Pulitzer Prize finalist and twice-winner of the Robert F. Kennedy Journalism Award, cartoonist and writer Ted Rall is one of America's most widely syndicated journalists. **To Afghanistan and Back** is Rall's eighth book, coming on the heels of the widely-acclaimed graphic novel **2024** and the influential political manifesto **Revenge of the Latchkey Kids**. Born in Cambridge, Massachusetts and raised in Kettering, Ohio, Rall graduated from Columbia University with honors in history in 1991. His trips overland from Beijing to Istanbul and along the Karakoram Highway in Kashmir were chronicled in pieces for *P.O.V.* magazine; Rall's journey to Afghanistan was his fifth adventure in Central Asia. His "Stan Watch," a summary and analysis of Central Asian news, has been broadcast frequently on NPR and the BBC. He lives in New York.